PLANTING AN INHERITANCE

Other books by Edwin A. Peeples

Play
Fantasy on an Empty Stage

Novel
Swing Low

Nonfiction
A *Professional Storywriter's Handbook*

Children's novels
Blue Boy
A Hole in the Hill

PLANTING AN INHERITANCE
Life on a Pennsylvania Farm

Edwin A. Peeples

STACKPOLE
BOOKS

Published by
STACKPOLE BOOKS
5067 Ritter Road
Mechanicsburg, PA 17055

Some of the material in this book was adapted from articles originally published
in *Country Journal* magazine; in *The Green Scene*, the magazine of the Pennsylvania Horticultural Society; and in *County Lines* magazine. The author is grateful to these three publications for permission to use their material in this book.

Printed in the United States of America

10 9 8 7 6 5 4 3 2 1

First Edition

Library of Congress Cataloging in Publication Data

Peeples, Edwin A. (Edwin Augustus)
    Planting an inheritance : life on a Pennsylvania farm / Edwin A.
Peeples.—1st ed.
        p.   cm.
    ISBN 0-8117-1206-0
    1. Farm life—Pennsylvania—Chester County. 2. Gardening—Pennsylva-
nia—Chester County. 3. Peeples, Edwin A. (Edwin Augustus)—Homes and
haunts—Pennsylvania—Chester County.
    I. Title
    S521.5.P4P43 1994   94-11700
    635'.09748'13—dc20   CIP

To
ERNESTA DRINKER BALLARD
who, while raising the Pennsylvania Horticultural Society
to exceptional solvency and international fame, found time
to encourage me to write about horticulture

Contents

ᕽ

STANDING ON THE THRESHOLD

❧

A Farm Is an Open Door

Nearly fifty years ago, my wife, Mimi, and I moved to our sixty-five-acre farm in Chester County, Pennsylvania. We were fleeing urban living and suburban pursuits to seek, in a rural environment, new sets of values. The most important value we sought was permanence.

I had an additional ambition. I wanted to create a fine house with a big library that might, in a modest way, become a showplace surrounded by parklike plantings. I had studied and admired the palaces, castles and great houses of the world. They showed how gracious living demanded generous spaces indoors and broad expanses outdoors. They also showed by their long history and atmosphere of permanence that the best estate to leave to one's heirs was one that you planted and built.

Mimi and I had little money, and the salary I could command was small. The only way we could own a great house would be to find a farm at a bargain price and do most of the alterations with our own hands.

We found such a farm. It was a bargain because, when we bought it, the title was cloudy. The house had the stark, forsaken look usual to abandoned railway stations. It was sound enough, and habitable in a rudimentary way: a stone box of comforting antiquity. It had been built in 1797, the year that Coleridge wrote *Kubla Khan* and the composers Donizetti and Schubert were born, the year Napoleon defeated the Austrians at Rivoli. Over the years we have come as near to converting it to match our dreams as anyone ever does with a house and grounds, for such a project is never finished so long as the owners live.

I was not a farmer. I had no ambition to become one. So our residence had to be within feasible commuting distance of jobs. Our farm was, just barely. The trip to a Philadelphia office by car, train and foot was more than an hour each way, but the joy of life in the country was worth the ordeal.

No matter what strife and stress I endured in the city, I could find refuge from it on our farm. The country had its own sets of strife and stress, of course, but they were so different, they were relaxing.

Our farm opened the door upon basic concerns that everyone should ponder regularly. No amount of mewing oneself up in buildings of glass and steel, plastic and aluminum, protected by floors of terrazzo and concrete and bitumin, can eliminate one's need to be in accord with nature. Let a man fail to face this responsibility or to understand how nature functions and inevitably he will be caught off guard by such catastrophes as a Mount Pelée or a Mount St. Helens, or by earthquakes or floods or forest fires, droughts, hurricanes, famines or blizzards. He will also be surprised by such manmade outrages as nuclear threats, acid rains, contaminations of water and earth by toxic wastes, the perils of overpopulation and what happens to the herds of white-tailed deer and the gaggles of Canada geese when you kill off all the predators.

The interface with nature is not on Main Street nor on an interstate route nor in a suburban shopping center. It is in the country lane, the small brook, the field of clover, the marsh and the berry patch. Here the barometers are delicate and highly sensitive to change. Here the litmus papers are the leaves. I was glad to be, at last, on my own personal interface, even if the best telephone service we could get was a twelve-party line.

As soon as the phone was installed, I called the secretary of Pickering Hunt, whose country we had invaded, and invited the hunt to draw our covers. This was not so odd an act as it sounds. Our invitation established our proprietorship and, in effect, our peership with influential people in our neighborhood. It conveyed, further, that we understood proper protocol and thus might be civilized. We would reap other advantages. Where hunts ride regularly, strangers on dubious errands feel uneasy and tend to flee. The hunt, itself, is beautiful to watch, the horses and hounds being natural creatures in fluid movement.

∾

When I was in grammar school, during the 1920s, my class heard terrifying tales about how rapidly our forests were disappearing. We had cut them first to fuel steam locomotives, then to build houses and buildings and now, most profligately, to make boxes and crates for soaps and fruits, vegetables and fowls and pretty well everything else that had to be shipped. Virgin forests had once covered our nation with trees whose trunks, at breast height, were three feet or more in diameter. Never again would we see such trees.

Our farm taught us that much fine wood remained and more was growing. Profligate wood cutting for packing material had ceased by World War II. Industry had found other materials—corrugated board, plastics, metal—that worked better and cost less. As time passed, I saw more and more trees as large as virgin timber had been. Each of three oaks across the road from the end of our lane was eighteen inches in diameter when we arrived. Forty years later, they are nearly two yards in diameter and are still in good health. If some storm or some idiot doesn't fell them, they should outlast me by several decades, and my arrival and departure will have been only incidents in their longer history.

As we explored our twenty acres of wood, we found more healthy trees of similar size. Interest in our wood brought our first encounter with a horticultural subject. We invited a forester to counsel us about our woodlot. His verdict: for a woodlot it had too much silver beech and dogwood. He, himself, loved silver beech and thought few other sights so stirring as the vigorous stand we had in our wood. But beech and dogwood were spreading trees. They shaded down saplings of such good hardwoods as oak, poplar, ash, cherry and sweet gum. So! What we ought to do was cull the beeches and the dogwood.

A shortage of money saved us from this folly. I hadn't the time, the energy or the skill to fell half an acre of mature beech trees, and I hadn't the money to have them felled. So I left them, and they did no harm at all. They have gone on growing, and they light our forest with a glow of silver trunks.

We learned an important truth from this. A farm is like a large, raw diamond that must be studied before it is cut. The worst thing anybody can have, when he buys and takes up residence on a farm, is a lot of money. If he can wave the wand of a big bank account, he will be tempted to wade in, and to buy other people to wade in, and wrench everything into a completely new shape. The result will be a disaster.

Having no bank account to hire everything plowed, cut, drained, bulldozed and remodeled, all we could do was to go with an inquisitive eye into our fields and wood and count our natural blessings.

We discovered where the wild strawberry and the tansy grew. We found hedges of blackberries and black raspberries, a tentative new stand of tulip poplar carpeted with ground pine and punctuated with small volunteer junipers. All were being throttled by honeysuckle. So from time to time we spent a sunny Saturday removing the honeysuckle until the trees grew large enough to shade it down.

When we trod our pastures, they breathed fragrances of pennyroyal, peppermint and spearmint. We had four colors of violets, both true and false Solomon's seal, wild crab apples, wild cherries and wild grapes, jewelweed to cure poison ivy, soapwort, jack-in-the-pulpits, butter-and-eggs and the blue of wild chicory mixed with the white of Queen Anne's lace.

The shoulder of a high hill, where much of our timber stood, rose between us and the prevailing winter winds. The farmer who had built our stone house had positioned it shrewdly, backing it against this hill for protection. He had shown the same wisdom in building the house. Its back was a solid wall, yielding no window or chink to the needling drafts of winter. That first farmer had to think of such things. All he had for heat was fireplaces that burned some of that virgin timber I had heard about.

∿

We came to the country at a time when everybody, weary from a depression followed by four years of war, felt a strong urge to try to be self-sufficient. I suppose wartime rationing stimulated this. For four years we had had to adjust to shortages of such goodies as butter, choice cuts of meat, sugar, soap, shoes, clothing, decent whiskey and wine, automobile tires and gasoline. The prospect of getting on a farm and raising enough provender to be sure of an abundance or two was appealing.

We yielded to this urge in many ways before we discovered what the Babylonians, Assyrians, Egyptians, Greeks, Romans and every other civilization had already discovered: the man who tries to be self-sufficient has no time left to be anything else. To supply human needs any more complex than those of the residual Incas in the Peruvian Andes takes more time than anyone has. Nevertheless, it is a good education to try.

Mimi baked bread. While we had them, we sheared our sheep and had blankets made from our own wool. Mimi raised ducks, geese and chickens for our own table with some eggs and poultry left over to sell. We grew and preserved cultivated fruits and vegetables, gathered and preserved wild fruits, nuts and herbs. We bought beef and pork on the hoof, had it slaughtered and quartered and suffered the consequences of learning to do our own butchering, wrapping and freezing. Because we had so little money, we made all of the early improvements and repairs on our house. From this we learned the meaning of sweat equity: that you can accumulate money value equal to the value of what your labor creates. This wasn't a bad investment in an inflating economy. It was a way to acquire wealth for those whom inheritance or war had neglected to make rich.

We learned a more important regimen that I hope we'll never have to use. We learned to do most of the chores we would have to do should war or some other catastrophe wipe out such essentials to civilization as electricity, gasoline, fuel oil and telephones.

∾

Even modest adventures in rearranging the grounds immediate to a house bring one into touch with horticultural matters. Thrifty housewives, yearning for beauty in the early days of our country, planted roses and other perennials for outdoor color and indoor decoration. We had inherited a bounty of these enthusiasms.

Many of our neighbors were members of the Pennsylvania Horticultural Society, employed gardeners and competed in the annual flower shows. We went to these shows as a kind of neighborhood cheering section and grew so hungry for horticultural lore that we also began to go regularly to Longwood Gardens and study what would grow where.

We discovered why people in southeastern Pennsylvania have always been so interested in gardening as to produce botanists like Bartram and McMahon, and great gardening families like the Morrises and the du Ponts. Our part of Pennsylvania shares with Virginia, Maryland and North Carolina planting zone 6, which means that we can grow hundreds of plants that ought not to survive at our latitude. Growing such plants requires work and careful judgment.

Most of our horticulture owed its existence to Mimi. She had always been interested in plants, having grown up on a farm, but she had no formal instruction. As she and I bought books on horticulture to build our library, Mimi took to the subject like a duck to water. She liked to read horticultural dictionaries and encyclopedias. Gradually she became authoritative on plants and developed a considerable vocabulary of botanical names. Fortunately, she also had a green thumb.

Our adventures taught us a crucial consideration in working on a country house and grounds. You have to think in a new set of proportions. A terrace twenty feet long and eight feet wide, for instance, is impressive space on a house in town or in the suburbs. On a country house, it is little more than an eyebrow. When we terraced around our house, we needed more than three hundred feet of wall, some of it six feet high.

After learning to think in these proportions, one's mind turns from small scale to the large, away from what one has planted and back to what nature plants. Although we can plant azaleas and rhododendrons in abundance, the beauty of the woodland walk, which we began in 1988, will depend, finally, upon masses of bloodroot, pinkster flower, Solomon's seal, violets, Dutchman's breeches, Virginia bluebells, columbines, wild phlox, wild orchids, wild ginger, ferns, hepatica and other native plants. The fortunate thing about a farm is that whatever wild plant you have at all, you generally have by the acre.

Such interests won't lead to the kind of farm I often saw, especially in the South, where I grew up. Bereft of tree or shrub, the houses on these farms stuck out of the landscape like naked thumbs. Chickens, ducks, and geese brooded on the front porch and kept it well coated with manure and feathers. To him who admires that kind of farm, I say strength to his arm.

I can't believe, though, that rural need mean rudimentary or that work with the land need be divorced from artistic interest in land and structures and the passing of life. Each year I watch from my front terrace as a broad panorama takes fire with the wild exultation of spring. The air grows restless. Streams pour rude and overflowing torrents into every valley. Lawns throb with the buzz of flies, and daffodils splash the pasture with spills of raw yellow.

The truck garden must be planted. The fragrances of new-mown grass and hay waft in, followed by the scents of cherry blossoms, lilacs, roses and honeysuckles. Fragrance is odd in the country. Whenever the temperature rises above freezing, something blooms. It may be only a small weed, but it issues its perfume and the bees find it. As summer ends, fruits and nuts, both wild and cultivated, must be gathered and preserved.

Spring and summer are so vigorous that autumn is a welcome relief. The air grows as still as a child listening. A chill creeps in. The green of leaves grows old and dark and dusty. Walnut and locust trees, their foliage fallen, look gaunt, but the other trees hold their masses of brilliance until the first hard frost. Then the leaves sift down, soft as a first snowfall, and lie in heaps of pure pigment: lemon yellow poplar, lime green mulberry, reds, hammered golds, the deep rose blush of euonymus. The sky, suddenly visible, is blue and clear and pierced with unshaded sunlight.

Snow leaves a leaf dry and uncovered. It springs up quickly in the first cold gale and flees across the smooth white snow, a small animal in a panic.

Watching such a leaf once as I walked a road, I composed these doggerel lines:

> *I shall hate to leave the earth,*
> *It's such a lovely place.*
> *What other world could ever have*
> *So beautiful a face?*

A Heritage of Ancient Elegance

People do not buy a farm without a future in mind. Some dream leads them on. Usually the dream grows out of the past. Ours did.

Mimi had grown up on a produce and dairy farm in New Jersey where nearly every action and every item was focused on farming. Mimi's grandmother yearned for elegances but all she managed was a large rock garden along the road. She built it and tended it herself. She read widely, and she taught Mimi to like reading. You could say that Mimi learned to love fresh air and open space combined with literacy.

I grew up in a bungalow in Atlanta, where I yearned for the country. The bungalow was half a block from a large park, Piedmont Park, and around the corner from the Piedmont Driving Club, which I could frequent because my father was a member. I thought how fine it would be to own a house like the club surrounded by a big acreage like the park with its big lake.

I learned to like large houses that were separated from the road by sweeps of deep green, closely mowed lawns and precisely kept gardens. At first I thought my adulation for these places came from an envy of wealth and position.

Gradually I realized that I admired the land and the lawns and the structures because of what they were. Their owners simply had the means to bring order to natural chaos. Beneath every thicket, copse and spinney, I believed, lay potential lawns; each tangled wood contained the trees for a romantic grove; each broad, muddy, giggling creek, the makings of a narrow, deep, blue brook, fairy-tale style.

∞

Philadelphians, both Quakers and others, had always shown skill for running country estates as self-sustaining farms. Many, no matter how wealthy they were, seemed to have the same inquisitive instincts as Benjamin Franklin. They liked to explore, to test, to try adventures in cultivating plants and breeding animals. Dairy farming had been the dominant profitable business until the 1950s. It and horse breeding were the main businesses of farms in our area when we arrived.

Our countryside was like the Cotswolds in England. We had rolling hills, ample rainfall and fine grass on a soil base fairly rich in limestone.

Our immediate neighbor to the east, Mrs. Fraley, had converted an eighteenth-century farmhouse, former post office and general store to a small jewel of a residence. She had, she insisted, only modest means for keeping her fifty-odd acres, but she afforded help. A black couple, Mack and Mary, had been with her for years. Mack was the active member of the couple. He did the mowing, kept sheep and sheared them, planted and cultivated fields, smoked pork and maintained flocks of the fowls he liked to cook and serve when Mrs. Fraley entertained, which was often. Favorite among these were guinea fowls that roosted in trees above the lane and set up a tumultuous squaggling when anyone drove in.

For all of being the least wealthy of her neighbors, Effie Fraley was the catalyst that homogenized the society. She had a knack for people and was young in heart. Although in her sixties, she formed a great affection for

Mimi, who was in her twenties. The two of them went constantly on adventures like two girls the same age. She introduced us into her circle.

Owen Roberts, who was Effie Fraley's close friend, lived behind us on his farm, Bryn Coed. A Welshman and a Supreme Court justice, he owned some two thousand acres and had two Scots gardeners to maintain his grounds. Bryn Coed was the epitome of an English country manor, and Roberts was wealthy enough to indulge his gardeners the cost of any change that seemed needed. When they all agreed that the arrangement and proportion of the terrace called for another tree, they moved in a thirty-foot pin oak. "I am too old," Roberts told me, "to expect to see a small tree reach the right size. So I plant my inheritance as I go."

The superb gardening of Justice Roberts's Scots provoked Effie Fraley. She said they had dug out every flower bed to a depth of three feet and replaced its soil with topsoil, peat moss and fertilizer. "I find a flower and get it to grow two-inch blooms in my garden," she said. "Then I give plants to Elsie Roberts and her gardeners put them in those beds and get four inch blooms!"

ॐ

The neighbors to whom Mrs. Fraley introduced us who influenced us most lived to the west of us: the Langhorne Dicks. They also owned several thousand acres. Hebe Dick had been raised mainly in Europe. As a child, Hebe had dressed in one of her mother's gowns and done a Toulouse-Lautrec fall down a long stairway. It had not dwarfed her, but it had left one leg six inches shorter than the other. She had to wear a shoe with a great thick sole to compensate. Despite it, she had an angelic face and one of the sweetest natures we had ever seen. She was the beneficiary of a trust that gave her a large income for her lifetime.

Langhorne Dick was a slight, raw-boned rasp of a man with a closely clipped skull and acute and debilitating arthritis. He appeared at table where he had been arranged in his chair in advance, like Mr. Smallweed in *Bleak House*. It was always startling to hear a man who looked so resolutely Anglo-Saxon speak excellent French.

The Dick house had the look and feel of rural France. Stands of trees that Hebe had planted, for instance, stood in rows like the trees planted in France after World War I, rather than in the clumps they would have formed voluntarily. Most of the furniture and appointments were French.

One entered her house through a square courtyard closed on the north by a stone drywall covered with succulent hen-and-chickens, *Echeveria*, and topped by a barberry hedge. A barn with a dark green door closed the south side. A wrought iron fence connected the barn to the wall, and a wrought iron gate in the fence admitted one to the terrace, much of which lay in the shade of a linden tree. A martin house stood in that shade and held throngs of noisy inhabitants. The house stretched away on the right. On the left, the terrace ended at what was called a ha-ha wall, confusingly defined by dictionaries as a sunken fence but actually an open edge; this ha-ha wall dropped six feet to the pasture. Why ha-ha? we asked Mrs. Dick. "Ha ha, if you fall off," she said.

It was a lovely way to have a pasture. The animals wandered about in plain view, but they couldn't wander onto the terrace. A variety of animals lived on the Dick pasture: pilgrim geese, Pekin and Muscovy ducks, bantams, a mixed flock of sheep, several steers and two Brown Swiss cows.

The pasture sloped to a pond. The pond was a residue of one of the many graphite and iron mines that had functioned in our area early in the twentieth century. We had a similar graphite mine on our farm: a deep and mystic tarn whose water was ebony except when autumn's leaf fall coated it with crushed gold. Mrs. Dick had had the near side of her mine bulldozed into two mounds, one on each side of a path that sloped to the water's edge. She called the mounds the elephant graves. From the ha-ha wall you could see flotillas of geese and ducks engaged in maneuvers.

We saw this pasture for the first time in spring. Clumps of daffodils bloomed all over it. An Aberdeen Angus steer scratched his back on a metal arch that looked like a Shinto gate. Each time he scratched, the arch doused him with insect repellent. Troops of ducks and geese marched about in opposite directions, and a newborn black lamb, its karakul coat still glossy, dozed beneath a daffodil blossom.

❧

Hebe Dick's farm epitomized everything we thought a farm ought to be: beautiful pasture, visible animals, a landscape like a tapestry, superb food, good books and good conversation. Among other things, it always had the natural abundance that seemed to me a farm's chief attraction. Stories I had read in grammar school spoke of cribs filled with corn, barns piled high with baled hay and bags of oats and barley. Farm kitchens always had a good wife who made preserves and pickles, canned vegetables and baked bread. Apples, pears and other fruits were there for the picking. One might want for many things, but one would never go hungry.

The Dick farm took this concept to high epicurean levels. The cellar, for instance, had a walk-in freezer. The one time I visited it, I noticed Ball jars filled with what I took to be preserved Elberta peaches. Were they?

"Oh, no!" Mrs. Dick said. "Duck eggs! Frozen duck eggs. They are so much better than hen's eggs for cakes and pastries."

Near where her land met ours, she had half an acre of asparagus that her farmer kept weeded and cultivated. For more than a month each spring, she could surfeit herself and everyone else with asparagus hollandaise. The milk from Brown Swiss cows is unusually rich in butterfat. Mrs. Dick had a cream separator to concentrate this richness into a cream so thick it poured like warm taffy over succulent desserts.

Hebe Dick was precise about the aging of her beef and lamb. She raised both and had them slaughtered and butchered. She taught us that mutton is not an age of sheep but a result of curing. Use the meat fresh and you had lamb, no matter how old the sheep had been. Hang it until the fat began to turn and produce flavor and you had mutton. For a *coq au vin*, she had the cocks killed on Wednesday and hung outdoors in a shed until Saturday morning to give them the flavor of game.

The big problem with all of this rural abundance was that it took a lot of money and a lot of good servants, which soon nobody had.

The servant turnover at the Dicks' was constant and produced endless anecdotes. The only long-term servant, the Japanese gardener, tended the terraces and the fruit trees. Mrs. Dick said he had been Christianized by missionaries. She wasn't sure what sect. Wesleyan Methodist, perhaps. He had no bath with his room, so she had given him a kind of potty chair and a wash basin. The maids, who lived on the floor below him, complained that at two or three each morning he would snap his potty chair lid several times and sing in a loud voice: "Jesus loves me, this I know…"

Hebe Dick needed servants, she could afford servants and, in Europe, she had always had servants. When she needed extra servants for a party in London, and Parliament wasn't in session, she simply sent around to the House of Commons. They had beautifully trained people who were delighted to get the extra work.

This confidence in what was available abroad produced some of Hebe's more startling adventures. Unable to find suitable servants in our domestic market, she conducted long and anxious correspondence programs to import people whom World War II had dispossessed.

It was a discouraging enterprise. Many Displaced Persons simply pocketed the passage money and never came. Others came and worked until they learned the language and the country well enough to get jobs in factories. The bright ones managed this in six months.

Three of Hebe's imports were bizarre. The first, a female chef from Normandy, came with her twelve-year-old son. The son was amiable enough, but he required a pony of Calvados brandy each morning for breakfast. He drank any other liquor he came across the rest of the day and spent the evenings roaring drunk.

Hebe replaced this combination with an English gardener whose wife was said to be a good housekeeper. When they arrived, Immigration gave them exhaustive physicals: urine, stool, hemorrhoids, everything. Hebe was delighted to be getting such healthy specimens.

Then it turned out that the wife couldn't remember anything, dropped dishes for no reason and had periods of glassy-eyed staring. Hebe asked the husband what was wrong. "Well, mum," he said, "she's kindly, but she was blowed out of our flat in an air raid and into the next block by a bomb and was give up. Then they put a metal plate in her head and it troubles her."

Later the husband complained of pains. What did he think caused these? "I'm a-feared, mum," he said, "it's me trepanning."

"You mean you've both got plates in your heads?"

"Yes, mum."

The most dismaying import was the Canadian housekeeper who could cook, sew, clean, launder, do everything. Her only condition was that she must bring her little boy and his puppy. After the son who drank Calvados, Hebe hesitated. But by then the servant market had grown so bad she was desperate.

She went to the Thirtieth Street Station in Philadelphia to meet this couple. The train was in and a great crowd had gathered to view a phenomenon. The little boy, a six-foot, three-inch spastic, was being unloaded by three porters and a brakeman. His puppy, who watched it all thoughtfully, was a St. Bernard the size of a Shetland pony. Mountains of luggage accompanied this group.

"I thought you said your little boy!" Mrs. Dick said.

"To me," his mother said, "he'll always be my little boy."

These problems didn't prevent Hebe Dick from serving a seated dinner for twenty each Sunday. She was, herself, a superb chef and often did the difficult preparatory work because she enjoyed doing it. For the last year she was in residence she invited us every Sunday. She assigned me the task of making the cocktails. She didn't approve of cocktails. They spoiled one's palate. But in deference to the era—and the needs of the men, you know—she allowed one round. One Sunday I misgauged and mixed about half a martini extra. I urged it on her.

"Dear me, no," she said. "I dassant. I rapes easy!"

The quality of food at those dinners defies description. There was scarcely an hors-d'oeuvre in the French repertoire that she didn't give us. There were wonderful simple dishes, too, such as sliced new potatoes that had been marinated overnight in a tarragon vinegar with parsley and olive oil. Hers was one of the few tables away from their places of origin where one could learn accurately the flavor and look of dishes that were quite exotic in those days and are rare even today, such things as *bouillabaisse* as made on the French coast, *cassoulet de Castelnaudary aux genets*, and a *coulibiac de saumon* incorporating sturgeon backbone as the jelling agent, all these flavored with herbs Mrs. Dick grew and, in season, accompanied by fresh asparagus hollandaise.

We learned from Hebe about *galantine de boeuf* and *coq au vin bourguignon* and were rewarded at the end of our tasty lessons with a rich dessert, such as a plum flan made with plums she grew, the slices spaced so regularly they looked as if they had been arranged with a compass. Over this we were urged to pour the thick Brown Swiss cream.

Because Hebe's friendships were international, the conversation at her table was in French, German, Polish and English, in all of which she was fluent. She sat at the head of the table and translated comfortably from language to language. When she found I shared her enthusiasm for unusually gamey pâtés, she seated me on her left hand.

After dinner we sat again briefly on the terrace, which the Japanese gardener kept colorful by replanting four times per year. He was not a gardener of the level of the Robertses' Scots gardeners, but he pruned the fruit trees, gathered the fruit, managed the vegetable and herb gardens and did the annual beds on the terraces. People with gardeners derived their guidance on such flower beds from the main conservatory in Longwood Gardens, where the season began with primroses, then worked through bulbs and a gamut of petunias, pinks, candytufts, zinnias, geraniums, marigolds, asters and chrysanthemums, concluding at Christmas with poinsettias.

That was the time that I tend to think of as B.I., Before Impatiens. In those days, *Impatiens wallerana*, cousin of the jewelweed, *I. pallida*, seldom appeared in gardens. The preferred bedding plants among those of us who did not run to hired gardeners were petunias, zinnias and marigolds. But petunias and zinnias were not entirely satisfactory because their blooming schedule was erratic. Marigolds were a bit late to bloom but continued solidly once they got started. They were, however, rather insistently orange and yellow. The first all-summer-long bedding plant to seize everyone's fancy was the wax begonia, *Begonia semperflorens-cultorum*, which had white, pink or red flowers on plants with green, russet or variegated leaves. These begonias were showy and are still great favorites. Combining wax begonias with impatiens, which come in all colors and bloom steadily and profusely, gives beds of brilliant colors that bloom from frost to frost.

❧

As we sat with Hebe Dick on her beautiful B.I. terrace, comfortably digesting an incredible dinner, we felt this was the way to live in the country, the way we wanted to live. We were grateful to experience at the outset the utmost that elegant taste could provide.

But we were not of the era of Hebe Dick nor of the means. What we did must not require servants and must be on a much smaller scale. Our house and grounds must be no larger than Mimi and I could plant, clean, mow, prune, and cultivate.

BEQUESTS
FROM THE PAST

Inherited Horticulture

What grows around a farmhouse, what was planted by previous owners, gives a kind of botanical history of what inhabitants liked and admired in times past. People may clean out a house until little residue remains of the former residents, but no one cleans out plants. Plants may be clipped, mowed, even plowed under and planted over. If they are indigenous, they will come back. This fecundity of the earth is marvelous to behold.

The first inherited plant that thrust itself upon us was matrimony vine, *Lycium halimifolium*, which some unknown person in some unknown past had brought to our Northeast from Europe or Western Asia. What an ugly plant! Why anyone would want it around was beyond understanding. Its arching, spiny branches were ten feet long and bore insignificant flowers of a dull lilac. I never found them with any fragrance. The plant was pernicious. It produced suckers everywhere, especially growing from clefts in boulders where it was hard to uproot. We needed nearly ten years to get rid of this pest. The only plant we ever found more difficult to eradicate was wisteria.

Another less-than-thrilling bequest was pampas grass, *Cortaderia sell-oana*, an enthusiasm of 1920s horticulturists. Pampas grass came to us from South America. Our horticulturists grew it as material for dry arrangements because it produced long beige spikes that lasted a great while. Our clump was large when we arrived. It kept getting larger. It wasn't dangerous or thorny. It just usurped a lot of prominent space and wasn't overly attractive.

Our clump of pampas grass grew five or six feet from an equally large buckthorn bush, *Bumelia lycioides*, where a family of foxes lived. Buckthorn is a fairly pretty shrub with long, bright green leaves and small white flowers that have four petals and no fragrance. In bloom, this bush was a great drift of white, but to keep it attractive we had to prune it constantly and remove cartloads of old wood. It and the pampas grass threatened to grow together into a large botanical goulash.

Much as we regretted disturbing the fox den that had given our farm, Vixen Hill, its name, we decided that we had better overwhelm the pampas grass and the buckthorn before they overwhelmed us. I took a cutter bar to them and kept mowing until they disappeared.

Those three were the only inherited plants we eliminated because we didn't care for them. We did lose our original peonies, a clump of pink and a clump of white. They grew where fill for our terrace had to go. We tried to save them by gradually building their soil level. When we had raised the level a foot, the plants died.

To recompense nature and the peony family, Mimi selected a dozen unusual varieties of peonies from catalogues. We planted these in a bed beside our barn. They are still one of our spring glories. For nearly the full month of May each year, we get masses of incredible cut flowers: huge blossoms of white satin, pink, red and white, and red. These cut peonies have such fragrance, purity and elegance that they make our ordinary rooms seem chambers in a palace.

ॐ

Modest and unobtrusive, small clumps of a not especially pretty daffodil dotted our pasture, our swamp and the borders of our lane. The outer petals were chartreuse and, although the inner petals were yellow, the green prevailed. The blossoms were neither really green nor really yellow. They were also double. No clear, crisp, yellow trumpet rose from their centers. Instead, they displayed a mass of shredded yellow like streamers in a party favor.

For years we treated these daffodils contemptuously. We seldom picked them, even though they had a faint but pleasant fragrance. We never hesitated to dig them up and toss them aside if they were in the way of some important planting.

No matter. They were accustomed to abuse. Wherever we tossed them, they came up to bloom any old how with gay abandon. They were the first bulbs up in the spring, rising in resolute clumps of dull dark green down one side of the pasture. The horses didn't eat them. Grazing animals do not eat bulbous plants. And being trampled occasionally by hooves didn't faze them.

I searched *Hortus Third*, *Gray's* and all of my other references for a name for this daffodil. The closest match I could find was *Narcissus pseudonarcissus*.

A newspaper article finally enlightened us: the daffodil was called Queen Elizabeth in England and had been brought to America by the early English colonists. It was pleasant to believe this flower may have been the earliest new planting on our farm. According to the *Englishman's Flora*, these wild daffodils, which bloom prolifically all over England, have a name that goes back through medieval Latin to the Greek *asphodelos*, the plant that legend says grew across the meadows of the underworld and belonged to Persephone, Queen of Hell.

∾

Our lilacs were also imports. Lilacs are said to have come from Asia, mostly from China, by way of Europe. Will Durant, in *The Reformation*, says lilacs came to us by way of Turkey: "Thence [from Turkish gardens] came into Western Europe the lilac, tulip, mimosa, cherry laurel, and ranunculus."

Our lilacs, one of the thirty species of *Syringa*, were *vulgaris*, a species brought in before extensive hybridizing produced so many exotic varieties. *Vulgaris* grew to twenty feet, had the eponymous lilac blossoms and, while it was in bloom, filled the air with an incredible perfume. Each time it bloomed I understood why I always choked up when I read the lovely lines from Alfred Noyes's "The Barrel Organ":

> Come down to Kew in lilac time, in lilac time, in lilac time.
> Come down to Kew in lilac time (it isn't far from London!)
> And you shall wander hand in hand with love in summer's
> wonderland;
> Come down to Kew in lilac time (it isn't far from London!)

We inherited three large bushes, two near the house and one in the lane. We thinned them occasionally. They bloomed better when we removed the old, heavy wood. We always had enough blossoms to cut each spring, cutting sparingly, bearing in mind that cutting this year's blooms also removed next year's buds.

∾

During our first year, I found in our wood a new flower. It was orange and visible from a great distance. Close up, it had six bright orange, pointed petals with red dots. It proved to be another Asian import, *Belamcanda chinensis*, the blackberry or leopard lily. The leopard came from the look of the flower; the blackberry, from the look of the seeds. This was the first flower I transplanted on our farm. My original plant has flourished for forty years in the place where I put it.

The most prolific flower, which we had in clumps everywhere, was the orange daylily, *Hemerocallis fulva*. It was hard to believe that any plant so vigorously naturalized hadn't been here all the while. Any piece of it, tossed anywhere, took root and produced, fairly quickly, a huge clump that only incessant mowing could eradicate. But daylilies came to us from Asia via Europe.

Times change and with them, the living world around us. We don't mourn what we've lost of our original plantings; we rejoice at what we have managed to keep. And we wonder what a future generation will make of what we leave.

26

The Tipsy Virgin and
Napoleon's Hat

Roses usually were the sweet conceits of a farm wife who wanted a pretty thing to look at, a pretty thing that had no useful function. Perhaps the forlorn rose that our predecessor bequeathed to us was such a plant. It was *Rosa hugonis*, Father Hugo's rose. Father Hugo, a missionary, discovered this rose growing wild in northern China in 1899, and botanists named it after him. Our *hugonis* clung perilously to the edge of a low stone drywall. Owing to its situation, it seemed ever-staggering and tottering like a drunk in a windstorm. The first time we saw it bloom, though, the yellow blossoms were so perfect, so exquisitely chaste, so contradictory of the shrub's reeling posture that I nicknamed it the Tipsy Virgin.

The Tipsy Virgin was a harbinger of summer: it was the first rose to flower each year, bursting into dense cascades of soft, primrose yellow blooms that blazed in the sunlight and sated the air with fragrance. The Bush-Browns, in *America's Garden Book*, said of this rose: "This is one of the loveliest plants known to cultivation, and no rose garden is complete without it."

It also turned out to be unusually durable. No pests or diseases attacked it, and it thrived in poor soil. The less we fertilized it, the better it bloomed. When we built our terrace and had to bury the original location of this rose, we transplanted it to the top of the new wall into soil that was largely hardpan. We lost most of the original bush during the transplant. No matter. In three years the transplant was bigger than the original. Later we transplanted it again, made the error of fertilizing it and almost killed it. Mercifully, something distracted our attention and caused us to neglect it. This restored it to flourishing health.

We should have stuck with such China or Bengal roses as the *Rosa hugonis* and the romanus rose, *R. rugosa*, or such wild roses as the dog rose, *R. canina*, and the burnet, *R. spinosissima*, or the moss roses, all of which might loosely be called original roses in the sense of having long histories, being pretty much pure rather than hybrid strains and being substantially pest and disease free.

The Greek poetess Sappho sang of the beauty of such roses in 600 B.C. The Egyptians cultivated roses. The rose was one of the first flowers to be domesticated, and this happened so long ago that its name is the same in nearly every language. Its shape has figured in every sort of design from architecture to pastry to textiles. But the first plant that the beginning gardener thinks of is the hybrid rose.

Hybrid roses have pedigrees, unusual shapes and exotic colors. The first one we tried was on the conservative side: 'Silver Moon', a climber for our new trellises that stood between our new French doors on our new terrace. 'Silver Moon' was a large, single, four-petaled white rose. When it bloomed, as it did most of the summer, it was gorgeous and breathed a delicious aroma of roses and lemon. But it grew so fast, in so many different directions at once and with such murderous thorns, that soon we couldn't get out the French doors. We were about to be mewed up, like Sleeping Beauty. We had to get rid of 'Silver Moon'.

Meanwhile, a thicket in our swamp thrust up a volunteer dog rose. We cleared around it. Encouraged, it grew to a considerable bush, a cloud of pink and white blossoms in the spring, a blaze of red hips in the autumn.

But the dog rose was really a by-blow. We hadn't cultivated the rose in the true sense. The true rose gardener raised floribundas and grandifloras, hybrid perpetuals, tea roses and hybrid teas in carefully managed rose gardens with perennial borders. We hadn't a suitable flat place for such a garden, but we did have a border on our front terrace that could accommodate six bushes. We planted 'Vogue', 'Fashion', 'Fusilier' and 'Mojave'. The first two were floribundas, the last, a hybrid tea. 'Fusilier' was a dramatic red rose that was brilliant red in warm weather and almost black in cool weather. I can no longer remember its type.

All of these roses were exquisite. They were also prey to every ill known to roses. Japanese beetles loved them. They teemed with aphids. Unless we covered them entirely with straw, cold weather killed them to the ground. Diseases blotched and perforated their leaves.

The true rose gardener expects these problems and is prepared and eager to cope with them. We were not true rose gardeners. With all of the other demands of a large property, we simply had too many things to do to provide the proper care for delicate roses. We neglected our special roses, and hard winters killed them.

☙

All this time in a bed at the edge of the pasture, our *Rosa hugonis* thrived with little attention beyond pruning. If only we could find other roses that would be as rewarding and undemanding as Father Hugo's, we might satisfy our longing for roses.

Into our yearning came a beautiful catalogue, *Roses of Yesterday and Today*, from Will Tillotson's Roses in Watsonville, California. This catalogue displayed moss roses, ten of them, saying of them that they were strong growers with above-average hardiness. All were bush roses and all but one, the 'Waldtraut Nielson', grew no taller than six feet. The 'Waldtraut Nielson' would go to ten feet or more.

The moss rose was a cultivation of the Victorian Age, when people liked elaborate architecture, clothes, decoration and, where feasible, flowers. Moss, itself, was an enthusiasm of the age. A proper garden ought to feature extensive stretches of moss to show it lay in dense shade, was well established and was not something put in yesterday. Indoors, moss carpeted bowls of cultivated flowers and garnished table decorations. What an appropriate milieu for a moss rose!

No one is clear where the moss rose sprang from. Twenty-four varieties were known before Queen Victoria ascended the throne in 1837. Moss roses must have failed to grow popular, for only two of the ten Tillotson listed were developed in the twentieth century. Judging by their names, most if not all were developed by the French.

The oldest and most dramatic moss rose, the common moss, *Rosa centifolia* 'Muscosa', has been tracked back to 1696. A clear pink rose, it was probably the rose from which modern moss roses evolved. The striped moss, which is crimson and white like peppermint candy, appeared in the early 1800s, followed in 1827 by the pink crested moss, 'Châpeau de Napoléon', Napoleon's Hat. The two more modern ones were the flesh-pink to deep salmon 'Gabriel Novelle' (1933) and the dusky pink 'Mossman' (1954).

The distinguishing characteristic of the moss rose is that its buds look like balls of moss with color peeping through. The buds continue to display moss until the bloom is fully open. Even then, turn the blossom upside down, and there is the moss.

The crested moss, the 'Châpeau de Napoléon', was one of the most startling of the moss roses. A large pink rose up to two inches in diameter, it bloomed all through May and June. Its mossy buds were shaped like the hat Napoleon is always shown wearing in the field. Although the buds seemed to explode into huge pink blooms, there was so much moss on the hat that much of it was still visible in a side view of the open rose. A bush covered with such hats in varying stages of opening was quite a sight. It seemed only proper to plant Napoleon's Hat next to our Tipsy Virgin.

To accompany these, we planted another moss rose, 'Salet' (1854). It was nearly as mossed as Napoleon's Hat but was a deeper pink and more fragrant. Writing in 1902 about roses for distilling perfume, Foster Melliar, a pharmaceutical chemist, said: "The real odor of musk is to be found only in 'Salet'—a perpetual moss rose."

'Salet' was not, however, the rose around which the French perfume industry grew in Provence during the thirteenth century. The perfume rose, known long before 1200 A.D., was *Rosa gallica officinalis*, the apothecary's rose. Thirty years ago, no one seemed to stock or recommend it.

The Tipsy Virgin, 'Châpeau de Napoléon' and 'Salet' gave us rose blossoms from late April until first frost. The blossoms were not always plentiful. Only 'Salet' bloomed after July first, but we always had at least one blossom and were reasonably content with our limited choice.

We dreamed, occasionally, of trying another moss rose or two. We were tempted by 'Alfred de Dalmas' (1855), a pink; 'Comtesse de Murinais' (1843), a white; 'Nuits de Young' (1851), a dark grape purple; 'Gloria de Mousseaux' (1852), flesh pink; 'Deuil de Paul Fontaine' (1873), crimson-black, purple and brown-red; and 'Mme Louis Leveque' (1874), soft lilac-pink.

Our conclusion about roses for such gardening people as we, whose interests were wide-ranging and whose time was limited, was that a selection of moss roses along with a Father Hugo's or one of the other China roses—*Rosa rugosa chinensis* var. *minima*, say, or *R. xanthena*—made an ideal and carefree combination.

Should we elect presently to plant a *Rosa rugosa*, a deep carmine rose that blooms all summer, we would have an additional bounty: the hips. Robert Rodale, founder and editor of *Organic Gardening*, wrote in 1958: "No food produced in the garden comes anywhere near having the concentrated food value of rose hips, and *rosa rugosa* hips are more valuable than those of any other rose."

Pomes, Pears and Peaches

All farmers leave for their successors
fruit trees, especially apple trees. Because such trees beget volunteers of
varying quality and identity, apple trees show up in hedgerows everywhere.

This fecundity of the apple probably stimulated the legends of Johnny
Appleseed, who was supposed to have walked our nation sowing the seeds
that gave us our apple trees. A pretty thought. But apple trees from random seeds do not good apples bear, save by accident. Two volunteer trees
that reached bearing age on our farm had apples as hard as raw potatoes
and equally tasteless. You could have played an inning of baseball with
one. Not even a horse would eat such apples.

Two other volunteers on neighboring farms had no crisp stage. Their
apples went from green to mush and had so little juice they were useless
for cider.

We inherited six cultivated apples. The naming of apples has grown
confusing enough that few will try to sort them officially, so I'll call ours by
the names the farmers gave them.

At the top of our orchard, which ran up the hill behind our house, stood a tree of what were called Summer apples. Late in June it bore a brilliant red and green apple of moderate size with a satin-smooth skin and very white flesh. It was tart and juicy but had to be eaten at once. It wouldn't keep a week.

The next bearer to ripen fruit was a delicate tree at the low end of the orchard. It bore what we were told were Lady apples: slightly larger than golf balls with red tops and yellow bottoms and quite sweet and juicy. Side by side were a Red Delicious and a Yellow Delicious. We learned how a Yellow Delicious that had ripened on the tree could taste enough like bananas to warrant the name banana apple.

Our two biggest bearers were a Baldwin and a Smokehouse. One year we got enough apples from these two trees to make ninety gallons of cider at an average yield of four gallons to the bushel. The Baldwin apple was about the size of a baseball and firm and crisp. It had a white, sweet flesh and was exceptionally juicy. The tree itself, which was not in the orchard but beside the front pasture, looked as if only nature had pruned it. The trunk rose bare to a height of eight feet, where it issued a cloud of branches. Above the cloud, the trunk rose another ten feet to a large parasol of branches. These Baldwins were late apples that didn't ripen to full juiciness and sweetness until after first frost.

The Smokehouse ripened earlier. It was a yellow apple and an ugly one. No matter how much we sprayed, its skin was rough, blotched and unsightly. Full ripeness brought to it a faint blush of pink or red. Its flesh had the soggy yellow look of overripe sugarcane. Its shape was flat, like a flat onion. But flavor? It had one of the most delicious flavors I have found in an apple: winey with perfumes of flowers.

❧

While our three sons were young, we picked apples and went cidering every year, taking eight to ten bushels of apples in our pickup truck, our boys lounging in back with the apples and gazing up into overhanging trees as we went.

The cider mill, run by Steve Lloyd, was a shed full of ancient equipment, wasps and yellow jackets. Trucks and people stood in line in the stinging golden sunshine of autumn and waited to have their apples pressed, to pour their apples into the endless belt that took them up to a snarling grinder, to watch the apple mush drop into canvas squares held in wooden frames, each square folded like an envelope when full and topped with a wooden grating, the envelopes and gratings piling high. Finally Steve started the press, ca-chugg ca-chugg ca-chugg, pressing the stack of envelopes and gratings against a steel plate. The cider flowed slowly at first, then cascaded in a honey-brown cataract into a metal trough. Pumps took it to the adjoining bottling room and sluiced it through a cylinder of fine screen that, turning constantly, sifted out the remaining dregs and rolled them into brown cylinders while people filled their gallon jugs and barrels from a bank of taps.

We brought our cider home and tried all kinds of uses for it. The boys drank gallons of it while it was fresh and liked it even better when it began to ferment and develop an effervescence and a tangy taste. We bought a charred fifty-gallon former whiskey barrel, filled it with cider and added sugar and raisins. We closed the bung with a beanbag full of dry sand, which would let air out but not in, and produced a decent apple equivalent of Sauterne. The next time we tried to make wine, either the apples were poor or we did something wrong. The result was undrinkable. We couldn't bear to empty the barrel, so we left it in the upper floor of the springhouse. It froze. I drained off the unfrozen liquid. It was sickeningly sweet but about forty proof. Some radio performers who visited us liked it and got smashed on it.

During these years we had our apples sprayed twice each season: once with sulfur, once with nicotine. This was not wildly successful. Apples needed four or five sprays per summer, and some of these, the commercial sprayers insisted, should be complex chemical sprays. We couldn't yield to this because such sprays killed birds. So we stuck to our two sprays, and although they didn't give us bite-free fruit, they did assure us of a good crop each year, most in fine condition.

A Russian neighbor of ours, Nina Brodovitch, insisted that the way to keep apple trees bite free was to mulch them with stones. She had circles of what looked like cobblestones beneath her trees, and her apples did seem to have fewer bites.

∽

Our predecessor farmers had also left us some other fruit. We had one clingstone and one Elberta peach tree, each battered and struggling, but each a bearer. We got a dozen or so peaches each year.

The two peach trees stood with a Bartlett pear tree where the long slope against which our house was built leveled into our front pasture. A three-post arbor of Concord grapes ran along this line, and the line itself was a favorite habitat for wasps, yellow jackets, hornets and carpenter bees, because masses of fruit rolled down and accumulated beneath the arbor. We divided with these insects the peach crop and the Bartlett pears. One or two years we got enough grapes for wine and jelly.

Mainly, though, the fruit slowly fermented. Several years I was fascinated with the effect this fermenting fruit had on the insects. They seemed to get drunk on it. They flew about heedlessly, colliding with me and other objects, fell on their backs and writhed and buzzed awhile in bibulous ecstasy. The bacchanal went on until the night the first frost killed most of them. I like to suppose that being drunk, they died happy.

As our sons grew up and went away, we had no use for so many apples and we stopped spraying. By then a dreadful disease, which we knew as fire blight, had killed the Lady apple, the Red Delicious, the Bartlett pear and both peach trees. Trees struck by fire blight develop split, dead limbs with dry, peeling bark as if the tree has been scorched in a fire. Ultimately the tree dies.

Natural forces saved the Baldwin from this indignity. One autumn equinox a storm brought it down.

THE TREES
AROUND US

Black Walnut:
A Tree of Mixed Blessings

One of the most impressive sights that greeted us on our farm was a black walnut tree thirty feet from the northeast corner of the house. It was eighty feet tall and fifty feet across the broadest point in its candelabra spread. It dominated and, from some aspects, seemed larger than the house, a kind of mothering presence. It was comforting. At the same time, its imposing structure was formidable and a touch frightening.

A local farmer called us lucky to have this walnut where it was. Walnuts, he said, owing to their wide limb spread and their sap's ability to conduct electricity, were the best lightning rods you could have. Circumstantial evidence has supported this thesis. During the forty-eight years we have spent in our house, it has never been struck by lightning.

Juglans nigra, we noticed, was a predominant tree in our area. Then we noticed it was a weed tree. Black walnuts planted themselves wherever a nut lingered: in our vegetable garden, in our rock garden, in hedges of yew, holly, barberry and privet, in pastures, if we didn't keep them mowed, and anywhere else the sun shone and the only competition was bushes and shrubs. The one place I saw few volunteer black walnuts was in the midst of our wood. Some mature walnuts grew there, but they must have sprung up before the other trees shaded the undergrowth.

The black walnut tree has many disadvantages. It is one of the last trees to get foliage in the spring, one of the first to lose it in the fall. Any walnut near a house poses a serious bombardment problem. The nuts come near being lethal. They are, in their husks, three inches in diameter and about as hard as a golf ball. One of these, dropping from fifty feet, can deliver a stunning blow. Our walnut was near the path to our front door. Every autumn Mimi had to wear an old World War I helmet to protect her head. From time to time she took a direct hit that rang the helmet like a gong. The rest of us, who made fewer trips, shielded our heads with our arms and ran.

The nuts clutter paths, drives and lawns and are painful if you catch one on your instep. If crushed when green, they yield a yellowish juice that quickly turns a purple black—what the Mikado had in mind when he sang of "permanent walnut juice."

The leaves also contribute to the litter. A walnut leaf is not merely one of the oval lanceolates that grow in a fernlike arrangement suggestive of the foliage in a Japanese print, but the complete combination, stem included. These composite leaves, one to two feet long, may contain eleven to twenty three-inch-long lanceolates, which are smooth, bright green, sharp-toothed, shiny above and hairy beneath. Early autumn brings down the lanceolates, and the first hard frost brings down a deluge of stems.

∽

A startling aspect of the black walnut is its effect on surrounding vegetation. Beginning in 1939, Professor Maurice G. Brooks, of the University of West Virginia, and his staff studied hundreds of black walnuts in West Virginia, Virginia, Maryland, Ohio and Michigan. They were exploring the toxin in the sap of black walnut, juglone, or alpha-naphtha-quinone.

Brooks confirmed a fatal antipathy of black walnuts toward apple trees but could not find any adverse effects on peach, cherry, plum, pear and quince. He found also that black walnuts are usually fatal to such erica-ceous plants as rhododendron, azalea, blueberry and laurel, to most of the pines, and to hemlocks, arborvitae, sweet gum, American holly, persim-mon and black ash. Black walnuts also kill tomatoes and potatoes. In the root spread of a black walnut, blackberries die; black raspberries thrive.

The fatal attack, when there is one, comes from the juglone and seems to occur only when there is contact between the roots of the black walnut and those of the victim. Brooks discovered occasional apple trees, azaleas and rhododendrons growing under black walnuts and supposed, at first, either that they disproved his other findings or that they had devel-oped some special immunity. In every instance, however, a rock formation or some other barrier had shielded the vulnerable roots from those of the black walnut.

One might expect black walnut root systems to increase the acid condition in soil, as do other roots. Instead, they make the soil more alka-line. The first tree Brooks's group tested was a seventy-foot specimen in a pasture with poor, thin soil. The soil outside the sixty-foot perimeter of the tree's roots had a pH of 5.1; inside was a more alkaline 5.8. In limestone and calcareous shale terrain, which already had a pH of 6.1, walnuts increased the reading only to 6.4, but in very acid soils of 4.5 or lower, wal-nuts increased alkalinity dramatically.

The pH boost does seem to have another, beneficial effect. The orig-inal evidence of this appeared beneath that same seventy-foot tree in the poor pasture and has been resoundingly confirmed by all additional tests. The soil under walnuts is marvelous for growing nearly every desirable pas-ture forage—Kentucky bluegrass, timothy, fescue, clovers of every kind and mints—while, at the same time, discouraging such undesirable growths as broom sedge, poverty grass and blackberry. Usually the walnut root pattern can be traced exactly by the points at which one set of plants replaces the other. Whether this phenomenon is due entirely to the pH improvement or to other contributions from juglone is not clear, but the evidence is conclusive: anyone who wishes to improve the quality of a poor pasture would do well to plant its borders in black walnut.

Many trees tolerate the black walnut without difficulty: hawthorn, for instance, American elm, beech, locust, tulip, white oak and red cedar. Also, certain ornamental shrubs will grow on black walnut root systems: *Cornus racemosa* and three varieties of euonymus, *Euonymus alatus, E. europaeus* and *E. vegetus.*

∾

The black walnut is an American tree with a beautiful wood grain and a nut that has a powerful acidic flavor. It is hardy to zone 4 and can grow to heights as great as a hundred feet. The twigs begin velvety brown and become smooth and light brown. The bark on old trunks grows scaly. The thick, dark brown scales break into prominent ridges and resemble the hide of an alligator. The branches are coarse and wide spreading.

Black walnuts grow in rich soils from northern New England through southern Canada west to South Dakota, south to central Texas and east to central Georgia, reaching the Atlantic coast in South Carolina. The tree does not grow at high elevations, but it is well distributed in rich lowlands throughout its growing area.

Black walnut grows in an odd way. The tips of twigs do not continue in the direction in which they start. Each spring, new growth begins at a bud several inches back from the terminal and on the underside of the twig. This curious process produces branches that zigzag instead of growing straight.

Black walnut trunks commonly reach diameters of two to four feet. Trunks as large as six feet are not infrequent. The usual heights are seventy to eighty feet, but 150-foot trees have been reported. These sizes in a wood that is heavy, close grained, strong and beautiful make black walnut valuable for furniture, interior paneling and gunstocks.

The Assyrians used walnut furniture. So have most nations since, but it is difficult to determine which of the sixty species of the family

Juglan daceae was predominant. *Juglans* is a contraction of *Jovis glans*, "the nuts of Jupiter." The Britannica suggests that *J. regia*, the common walnut native to the mountains of Greece, Armenia, Afghanistan and the northwest Himalayas, was the original furniture wood, for this was the tree cultivated in most temperate zones for timber and edible nuts. The Romans are said to have introduced *J. regia* to the British Isles, where it became English walnut.

Both Spain and Portugal used walnut in furniture before the fifteenth century, but oak continued to be the preferred wood in England until near the end of the century. Then walnut supplanted oak. The oiliness of walnut made it a smooth, dark wood that looked like bronze. Because its grain was finer than the grains of other woods, it was easier to carve into the figures that people wanted shown in relief on their furniture. Walnut grain has a varied pattern and juxtapositions of light and dark. As it ages, the darks grow almost black while the lights retain a certain golden creaminess. Although staining walnut can give it a variety of finishes, Mimi found that black walnut achieved its greatest beauty if rubbed with a mixture of linseed oil and turpentine.

No one seems to draw a distinction between the grains of *Juglans regia* and other walnuts and *J. nigra*, our black walnut. The implication is that though the flavors of the nuts are quite different, the beauty of the wood is close enough to be interchangeable. Black walnut is, in any case, the dominant furniture walnut in America.

What about these nuts of Jupiter as produced by *Juglans nigra*? The English walnut, most prevalent at Christmas season, has a flavor and a kernel somewhat like a pecan. This is not surprising. The walnut and the pecan belong to the same family. The black walnut's kernel is somewhat fatter but almost identical in shape to that of the English walnut. But where the shell of the English walnut is clean, thin and biscuit colored, the shell of the black walnut is brownish black, thick, grooved all over and heavy with stain. The nut itself is oily and so overpoweringly strong that few like its flavor.

Even so, there are some dessert recipes for black walnuts, chiefly icings for cakes, that dilute the flavor enough to make an appetizing confection.

Once there was a tasty commercial candy, Walnettos, based on black walnuts. Our friend Bill Dall told us that Worcestershire Sauce was make by picking walnuts when they were the size of green olives and pickling them in vinegar. One weekend when he was visiting, we tried it. It wasn't successful. I think we got the nuts too large. More important, I suspect the recipe called for English walnuts instead of black walnuts.

Walnuts commence to fall in September and continue until first frost. The nut is encased in a smooth, thick outer husk, which begins a light green filled with bright yellow pith and juice, and speedily turns brown, then black. The odious part of getting black walnut meats is getting rid of this husk. Years ago, when we gathered walnuts in quantity, we ran them through a hand-cranked corn sheller. It did a fine job. More recently, our needs being less, we toss the nuts into the drive for cars to run over or, wearing old tennis shoes, crush off the hulls with our feet. Once the hulls are off, the nuts should be dried. Else the shelling will be a hand-staining experience.

Whereas the English walnut can usually be opened, as pecans can, by squeezing two nuts together, the only way to open a black walnut is with a hammer and a hard surface. I use a slab of slate. For all of the nut's toughness, however, proper tapping with a hammer will allow the sheller to get a good many whole or nearly whole nutmeats. Black walnuts yield a good deal of meat. A half gallon of nuts will produce about a pint.

Even for those who take their black walnuts straight and love every bite, it is well to let the nuts dry after they are shelled. All nuts are produced, as coconuts are, by the congealing of a kind of milk, but where other nuts set to reasonable dryness, black walnuts seldom seem to. Probably because of their high oil content and impenetrable shells, they come out moist and limp.

To reduce their flavor, I modified a procedure that my sister had sent me to use with pecans. The procedure for pecans was to bring a saucepan of water to the boil, put in the pecans, bring back to the boil and boil one minute, drain and dry for one and a half to two hours in a 200°F. oven. I thought black walnuts would need more time, so I upped the boil period to five minutes. The liquid I boiled off was the color of coffee. The flavor of the walnuts, although still powerful, was considerably reduced.

∾

The great value of black walnut is as a wood for furniture, paneling and veneer, not as nuts. Where the tree is indigenous, as it is in Chester County, Pennsylvania, producing a good crop of furniture wood is mainly a matter of managing volunteer trees as they grow. Elsewhere, in the great geographical area where *Juglans nigra* will grow, evidently some planting is needed. A friend in Connecticut, to whom I described black walnut as a weed tree, wanted to come down for some weeds.

As they grow, walnut trees should be pruned regularly. Left to themselves, they branch and fork at odd levels, producing random knots and tortured grains, which are attractive to cabinetmakers who like to work with rich, complicated burls, but not to the best market, the lumber and plywood industry. That market wants a straight bole twenty to forty feet long with a midpoint diameter of twenty-four inches measured with calipers beneath the bark. Such a log will yield a thousand board feet of usable lumber. Obviously, each generation must produce the next generation's cash crop of walnuts, for a tree must be seventy years old or more to yield a valuable log. Prunings of large limbs will yield four- to six-inch logs. If no craft use is available for these, they will make a firewood that burns a long time and yields a smoke that smells like dried tea leaves.

Mimi and I have cultivated and pruned a fair number of our volunteer walnuts, and we inherited some decent timber trees. I doubt we would have cut any if a woodsman hadn't come seeking trees when our cash was short. All of our trees could have stood more growth, but three in a dense wood were suffering from the competition. Each of these trees had had fencing nailed to it. They must have been at the edge of a field or pasture.

The practice of hanging wire fence on living trees goes back to 1816, when a paper, read to the Philadelphia Agricultural Society, advocated planting walnut and cherry trees for living fence posts and harvesting their tops for firewood. There was only one long-term disadvantage to the practice that these country generations didn't anticipate. The iron in fencing reacts with the sap of walnuts to produce iron salts, which are blue. These salts discolor the largest section of the trunk.

Because our own problem is, often, getting rid of walnuts, we have learned other facts. One is that you cannot kill a walnut by girdling it. We girdled three, and they continued in rude good health until we cut them down. You also cannot kill them by lopping off their tops. We have topped a walnut near our barn every four or five years for three decades. It simply grows another tree on the stump.

~

What finally happened to our original walnut? It developed a bear hole and threatened to fall on the house. So we sold it to the woodsman, but not until we made certain that other, younger walnuts in the woodlot directly behind our house were ready to take over the job of being our lightning rod.

Hickory, the American Tree

Hickory, dickory dock,
The mouse ran up the clock...

This American version of the English Mother Goose rhyme was, for many of us born before World War II, one of the earliest verses we knew. The original English version, however, had no hickory in it. It began, "Dickory, dickory...," *dickory* meaning boob or blockhead. It had no hickory because, when it was written, the word and the tree were unknown in Europe.

All of the main eight hickories and the numerous others called botanist's species were native to North America and only to North America. Native, in fact, to eastern North America.

Although some recent sources report an original hickory in China, *Carya cathayensis*, hickory has been so widely exported and transplanted since 1600 or so that such discoveries are suspect. During the eighteenth century, Thomas Jefferson, according to his diary, constantly shipped both nuts and trees to Europe.

The eight principal hickories fall into two categories, the true hickories, namely shagbark, shellbark, mockernut and pignut, and the pecan hickories, namely pecan, water hickory, swamp hickory or bitternut, and nutmeg hickory. The pecans bear larger and meatier—although often less edible—nuts and prefer lowlands and marshes; the true hickories bear smaller, hard nuts and like the higher slopes.

These purely American trees have threaded like a theme song through our early history, legend and literature, and their wood has tooled a whole era of civilization. Many of us had drubbed into us,

> Readin' and writin' and 'rithmetic,
> Taught to the tune of a hickory stick...

and my father used to call a whipping a little dose of extract of hickory.

The theme of hickory goes beyond commonplaces. Andrew Jackson was called Old Hickory to bespeak his toughness and durability when he refused to discharge his troops after the War of 1812, as ordered by the secretary of war. He marched them home to Tennessee along the Natchez Trace, shared their poor food and slept with them on the hard ground.

Indians used hickory poles to make brooms. French missionaries found the Iroquois fashioning brooms from single poles that were long enough to form both the handle and the brush. The Indians soaked one end of the pole until the annular rings loosened, then beat the wet wood with a wooden maul until it separated into strips that could be fashioned into a brush. The hickory used for this, *Carya glabra*, came to be called broom hickory. Indians used these brooms for messages. Placed across an Indian doorway, a broom said, "Nobody home."

Hickory tea in 1904 Arkansas meant a whipping; hickory in 1918 Martha's Vineyard meant a siege of rough and tempestuous weather. To inhabitants of 1931 Idaho, hickory was sagebrush, probably because it was also a very tough wood.

H. L. Mencken's *American Language* says the name *hickory*, borrowed from the Algonquin dialect, first appeared in 1634 and came from *powco-hiccora*, the name of a liquor the Indians in Virginia made by pounding the nuts and shells in water until they became a milky, oily slurry. The Indians boiled this slurry, then passed it through fine strainers. The resultant oily milk, sweet and rich as fresh cream, was an ingredient in much of their cooking. John Bartram found Indians so fond of this milk that some hoarded a hundred bushels of nuts at their dwellings.

The early colonists corrupted the name to pokickery or pohickory and applied it to the tree. Gradually they shortened it to hicquerry, heckory, then hiccory, which was what Thomas Jefferson called it in his letters and diaries.

That we, as humans, have come almost to the point of not noticing hickory is hardly surprising. We stand among trees as a child stands among adults at a party. A child sees only legs; we see only trunks: neither very interesting, neither doing much. During the autumn, when hickories drop their nuts, we notice these. Freshly sprung from their round husks, hickory nuts are nearly white and twinkle, stars strewn amid green grass or upon brown earth. The husks, which peel away in quarter spheres, have a brassy, musky scent that always seems to me to be the fragrance of autumn.

∾

I saw my first hickories on afternoon walks in the long and leisurely days of childhood. My sister and I gathered bags of hickory nuts and brought them home, having to crack them on a stone with a hammer. A pint of nuts yielded half a teacup of meats, but after our efforts, how delicious these were. The nutmeats breathed the fragrance of maple syrup.

Although few of us noticed the wood, during those days we were surrounded by hickory. In the 1920s, the items made of hickory were endless. The spokes, bodies, wheels, axles and tongues of wagons, sulkies and coaches were hickory. So were the bodies of early automobiles, streetcars and railway coaches. The handle of every hand tool was shaped from hickory's white sapwood. Many said that the American axe owed its high quality as much to its hickory handle as to its fine steel. Hickory was used for musket stocks, rake teeth, street brooms, parts for textile looms, dowels, tamping sticks, the bows of yokes, the handles of plows, and rungs for ladders and chairs.

Hickory dominated the sports world, being the wood of gym bars, billiard cues, the shafts of golf clubs, tent poles, lawn furniture and, before ash became the dominant wood for them, baseball bats. Some major-league bats are still made of hickory. American hickory was the wood most prized for skis. Weight for weight, hickory is stronger than steel, more elastic, less brittle and less heat conductive.

Possibly the most important application of the good bending qualities of hickory was in the shaping of wings and airfoils for early aircraft. Those planes needed a material that could be bent into sharpish curves and complex shapes, yet be tough enough not to break under severe impact. Hickory was the answer. The Wright brothers used it at Kitty Hawk.

Not only was hickory strong, it was one of the best fuels we had during the first two decades of our century. It burns brilliantly with a clean, nearly smokeless flame to produce an ardent heat. Heaviest of the common woods, at fifty-four pounds per cubic foot, hickory has the highest heating value per cord of any eastern hardwood. One cord of hickory is equal to 1.12 tons of coal, 175 gallons of fuel oil or 24,000 cubic feet of natural gas. One cord of air-dried hickory can yield about a thousand pounds of the finest charcoal, charcoal that is heavy, compact and long burning.

Man has always cured meat and fish by smoking them, but not until he found hickory did he manage to give them great flavor. This flavor comes only from the wood, which contains the flavor volatiles; hickory charcoal imparts no flavor.

Like most people, I had never actually identified a hickory tree any more than I had discerned which oaks produced the acorns I found strewn over the streets I walked. Only when we bought our farm did I look at hickory to know it for what it was. A hickory well over a hundred feet high, with a trunk two feet through, stood beside our lane. Another, even larger, rose from the middle of our pasture. I thought at first they were shagbarks. Their bark was shaggy enough. But after years of gathering and shelling their easily cracked and meaty nuts, I think they must be shellbark. Shagbark is much shaggier and its nuts are almost impossible to shell.

Shellbark hickory nuts are well worth gathering and shelling. I shell ours with an ordinary nutcracker. Shelling gives the hands an occupation like knitting where one can work and talk at the same time. I used it as an aid to giving up smoking.

Hickories flower in April and May. The trees are monoecious, with both male and female flowers on the same tree, so they are self-pollinating, and the nuts ripen in September. The nuts disperse by rolling down the slopes where the parent trees grow or by being carried off by animals. Squirrels, chipmunks and raccoons bury the nuts, which usually succeeds in planting them.

All hickories develop long taproots with few lateral roots. The taproot of a one-year shagbark seedling is a foot long. This taproot, which grows as rapidly as the tree, makes hickory one of the most wind-firm of all trees, and consequently one of the most difficult to transplant successfully.

The husks of all true hickory nuts separate into four valves or quarters, but these nuts do not appear until the trees are more than twenty years old. After they are forty, trees bear heavy crops at three-year intervals until they die.

Those who want good hickory nuts should buy young trees of developed varieties from nurseries, rather than try to transplant volunteers. A variety called Hales has nuts with thin shells that are easy to crack. Nuts from a variety called Kirtland are larger but more difficult to shell.

❧

Hickory goes incognito because for its first twenty years, it is a nondescript tree. In their youth, young walnuts, poplars and oaks show distinctive leaves, flowers and barks; molting trees, like sycamores and paper birches, begin to shed their bark in great sheets. But there stands the debutante hickory, smooth of bark, flowerless and fruitless, with a leaf structure that could be walnut except that the leaflets are huge. Hickories are not truly impressive until they are fully mature. Then they raise graybrown limbs like the groining in medieval cathedrals, reaching as high as 140 feet with trunk diameters of twenty to thirty inches, able to endure and thrive in temperatures from below zero to more than 100°F.

All of the eight hickories yield useful wood of similarly high quality, but only the shagbark and the shellbark have achieved commercial importance for wood. Our early woodcutters took from our abundant forests the finest and best hickories and from each log what they saw as the most desirable wood, the sapwood.

Hickory has two kinds of wood, the heartwood, light reddish brown to dark brown, and the sapwood, almost pure white. Both are tough, close grained and elastic, but the white sapwood, with its almost invisible grain, came to be preferred for tool handles. Customers erroneously thought it was stronger than heartwood.

It is a shame to discard any part of a hickory owing to unfounded prejudice. Hickories grow very slowly. The fastest grower, the shagbark, increases its diameter at an average rate of only 1.43 inches per decade. So our inheritance of hickory matures too slowly to allow any waste.

In forests or groves, hickory trunks rise fifty to sixty feet, bare of branches, and nourish themselves from an umbrella of leaves at their tops. Growing singly, in places like parks, hickories form rounded pyramids of foliage. In the spring, a shellbark about to put forth leaves looks as if it were covered with brilliant flowers. The outer scales of the leaf bud have fallen, allowing the inner scales to grow five inches long and two across. These scales have a leathery texture, are downy and beautifully fringed. Some are red, some salmon or yellow. Through these petallike scales the young leaves push, shiny, downy and bright green. The growing leaves turn dark green as summer comes, but the shade they give is dappled, not dense. Enough sunlight penetrates to encourage grass.

Come autumn, the leaves turn yellow. Briefly, green margins mark their veins. When these depart, the leaves drift down, crumpled sheets of gold leaf, to leave the gothic winter skeleton of the tree, a tortured figure in gray wrought iron.

It is comforting, in these days of uncertainty, to know that such a versatile resource abounds in park and woodland and increases steadily by an ancient planting ritual that James Russell Lowell observed:

> The squirrel on the shingly shagbark bough
> Now saws, now lists with downward eye and ear,
> Then drops his nut...

Black Locust, the Fence Post Tree

Most of the eastern United States was fenced with chestnut until the 1920s, not because chestnut was an ideal wood for fencing but because there was so much of it. It had grown so abundantly in every forest that it was used profligately. When I was a child in the 1920s and my father took me from Atlanta to Washington, I looked from the train windows at miles of snake or worm fence made by stacking six to eight rails in panels that had no posts. Being zigzagged, the meshed adjoining panels held the fence up. Almost all of these wasteful fences were chestnut.

By then disaster already loomed. We had imported chestnut blight from the Orient in 1904. Within forty years it had killed all of our chestnuts and left us needing a new fencing material, a wood that would serve well for fence posts. The farming world settled on black locust. The choice gave a post far better than any chestnut post. Even today, for long-term fencing locust makes the best post anyone can buy. It will outlast any other wood except osage orange; it will outlast steel, and it will outlast concrete.

My wife and I bought our first locust posts in 1950. At a nearby railroad stop, called Parkersford, an elderly man and his teenage grandson owned a locust grove and made a modest living cutting and selling fence posts. They were out cutting all day, so we picked up posts at eventide. Occasionally we had to wait at the rail crossing and let the daily mixed freight, pulled by a diesel with a dim headlight, potter through. Then, our way lit by a kerosene lamp, we went through a gloaming rich with woodsmoke and loaded locust posts.

The old man's locust trees had grown too large for full-round posts. They would have been too heavy and too expensive. Most had to be halved and a good many, quartered. The only full-round post we bought was to hold our mailbox. It was a foot in diameter. We sank it at the end of our lane in 1950. It was there until 1990, having survived five mailboxes and attacks with ball bats, other blunt instruments and—during the period when vandals were putting M80s in mailboxes—explosives.

Many of the split posts we sank for fencing that same year are still standing. The fencing has rusted away, but the posts endure. This is characteristic. There are records of locust posts that have lasted seventy-five years and of grape stakes only twelve square inches in cross section that have lasted fifty.

A commercial fence post should be seven to eight feet long with a diameter of four to six inches. For this one would need a tree five inches in diameter at breast height. Eric Sloane, author of many books on wood and woodworking, calculated that a two-hundred-acre farm should have twenty acres of top-grade locust to keep it fenced.

An alternative for one who could endure a few years of temporary fencing would be to plant young locust trees ten feet apart in a straight line and, when they grew large enough, nail steel fence to them. The iron salts might turn the wood blue, but locust is not a lumber wood, so it wouldn't matter.

Only two locusts are important for wood: black locust, *Robinia pseudoacacia*, and honey locust, *Gleditsia triacanthos*. Water locust, *Gleditsia aquatica*; clammy locust, *Robinia viscosa*; Elliott's locust, *R. Elliottii*; and bristly locust, *R. hispida*, are either small trees or shrubs. They and their hybrids are of horticultural value primarily as decorative plantings.

Black locust and honey locust look alike and, as fence posts, perform alike, but they are of different genera. Both have thorns. The thorns of black locust are paired; those of honey locust grow in clumps, each thorn several inches long. Woodsmen once used honey locust thorns for pins, spear points and animal traps. Both have compound leaves: lots of leaflets on a stem. Honey locust leaves, eighteen to twenty-two dentate (toothed) leaflets to a stem, can be twice compounded: a compound leaf growing out of a compound leaf. Black locust leaves have seven to nineteen nondentate leaflets on a stem and are not twice compounded. The roots of black locust fix nitrogen; the roots of honey locust do not. Each has white flowers on wisteria-like racemes. Those on the black locust bloom white or creamy white and are very fragrant; honey locust flowers, even more fragrant, are small and greenish. Each grows to eighty-foot trees and does it rapidly. In good soil, a black locust grows to forty-five feet in ten years, seventy feet in twenty-five years and eighty-five to ninety feet in forty years.

The shape into which a tree grows depends on where it grows: standing alone or crowded by other trees. A freestanding honey locust has a short trunk that branches at about twelve feet and rises to a broad head that is either rounded or flat topped. The common black locust has a divided trunk and scraggly branches. A new variety of black locust, called 'Ship-Mast', grows a single straight stem as tall as seventy feet and has the shape of a candle flame. Divided or undivided, black locust main trunks grow straight. This, and their ability to resist rot, is what makes locusts good for fence posts.

One reason for the durability of black locust may be poisonous materials in the inner layer of its bark. The predominant content seems to be protein. Black locust bark is the only bark that has yielded protein for isolation and study. The toxic factor in the bark, a combination of proteins, is called robin, after *Robinia*, just as the deterrent factor in walnut sap is called juglone, after the genus name *Juglans*.

When animals eat the locust bark, robin attacks their kidneys and bloodstreams to produce violent illness and, occasionally, death. The leaves, seeds and roots of locust also seem to contain robin in diminished amounts. Seeds, eaten freely by wildlife, produce no harmful effects, and the Germans used ground locust seeds as a coffee substitute during World War II. Boiling destroys the poisonous character of the proteins.

∾

The black locust and its family members, originally found only in North America, were first identified by Jean Robin (1550–1629), herbalist to Henry IV of France. With his son, Vespasian Robin, he imported and cultivated the first black locusts in Europe in the gardens of the Louvre and gave the genus the name *Robinia*.

Honey locust, long known in Europe and Asia but not officially named until after black locust, was called *Gleditsia* for Gottlieb Gleditsch, director of the Berlin Botanical Gardens, who died in 1786. This genus comprises, in addition to honey and water locust, a cross developed in 1949 called *Gleditsia triacanthos* var. *inermis* 'Moraine'. Moraine locust, which grows as rapidly as three feet per year to heights as great as a hundred feet, has no thorns, is wide spreading in form and is free from disease.

All locusts are members of the pea or pulse family, Leguminosae. The *Robinia* share a characteristic common to most of the family in having bacterial nodes that fix gaseous nitrogen on the roots. This nitrogen nourishes and stimulates the growth of other plants, including bluegrass and other pasture grasses. Hence, black locusts seldom form pure stands except as young trees on burned-over land. They grow from stumps, roots and old seeds and soon stimulate oaks, hickories and other trees. Because of its own rapid growth and strong root system, even in the shrubby stages, and because of the other growth its nitrogen stimulates, black locust is an excellent planting for gully control.

Disturbed areas in oak and hickory forests usually grow to black locust in the process of returning to oak and hickory. Locusts seem to arrive during the early stages of regrowth and are important successional species on disturbed sites. Indigenous throughout eastern North America, black locust is hardy from southern Louisiana to the southern shores of Lake Superior.

Most of our locusts appeared originally in our Appalachian and Ozark mountain ranges. Transplanting took the trees to all parts of the eastern United States and as far west as Oklahoma.

∽

The blossoms of both black and honey locusts appear between May and July. The brilliant white flowers of the black locust are easily visible dangling through the tree in snowy cascades. The greenish white blossoms of honey locusts tend to disappear amid the leaves. But the fragrances of both blossoms are so intense that you will know they are there, even if you can't see them. Failing that, listen for the commanding hum and throb of bees.

Few other trees are so useful to beekeepers as black and honey locusts. These trees bloom just before white clover, when few other flowers are available. Locust honey is rich and delicious.

Despite its early flowering, locust comes into leaf late and drops its leaves early, a characteristic that seems common among trees with compound leaves.

Black locust flowers mature to smooth, beanlike pods three to four inches long and about half an inch wide. The four to eight seeds per pod are dark orange, comparatively free of starch and rich in fat and protein. The fat, a kind of wax, makes the seed difficult to propagate because it keeps out water. Soaking the seeds in hot water, scarifying them or soaking them in xylene, ether, acetone or sulfuric acid will remove the waxy fat and allow them to germinate. Evidently the wax prevents the seeds from germinating before ambient temperatures are high enough. Undisturbed, the wax will protect the seeds for several years.

Locust can also be propagated with root cuttings, suckers and grafts. Once locust becomes established, it spreads rapidly through root sprouts that form clones the way aspen sprouts do.

Animals that eat the seeds spread locusts wherever growing conditions are favorable. Animal maws remove the waxy coating and replace it with nourishing manure. Cattle, deer, rabbits, squirrels and quail plant locusts in this way, taking the seeds considerable distances. Three mature black locusts grow on our front terrace. We planted them thirty years ago and they are fully seventy feet tall. For years we have found their seedlings three hundred and four hundred yards away.

Finding black or honey locust saplings in catalogues is difficult because there isn't much demand for the trees. This isn't because of aversion. People just don't know black locust and realize what an attractive tree it can be.

Sassafras: An Historic Fragrance

Country land has far more plants and trees than people and animals, and so has this book. The proportion, from a standpoint of giving the feel of things, is about right.

A farm has two kinds of trees: those that are indigenous and compose its woods, and those the owner plants. Our indigenous large trees were tulip poplar, black walnut, oak, maple, locust, wild cherry, dogwood, sycamore, silver beech and sweet gum. Once there had been great stands of white pine, but the early settlers cut all of these for lumber. We may, once, have had great stands of hemlock as well. They were gone, too, but both hemlock and white pine have begun to reappear in our hedgerows. Also lurking in the hedgerows I found a small indigenous tree, not often noticed these days, which has a fascinating story.

Sassafras.

I began to study it one morning in March when winter still gripped the dead world and the wet of rain lay slick and shiny on limbs and trunks.

Amid this bleakness, fat buds upon small trees with tortured limbs burst into chartreuse blooms. "Naked," to use the words of *Gray's Botany*, "in clustered and peduncled and corymbed racemes." The blossoms developed rapidly, drooped and were succeeded by candle flames of pale green leaves. That year those were the earliest leaves to appear. As I walked the road and looked across fields to the edges of woods, the random brush strokes of sassafras green were the prominent color in the tapestry. I was surprised and delighted to see what a lot of sassafras we had.

I first encountered the flavor and fragrance of sassafras at a baseball game in Atlanta in 1926. A stand in what was then Ponce de Leon Springs offered Hires root beer on tap. The evident thought was that those whom Prohibition had deprived of true beer might like a substitute that looked like the real thing even if it didn't taste like it.

The air around this stand breathed the lovely aroma of sassafras, and the venture might have succeeded, for it is in the South that sassafras grows best. Root beer failed to take hold, however, because Atlanta was the home turf of Coca-Cola, a beverage not so overpoweringly sweet as root beer and which, in those days, contained minute amounts of cocaine. If you drank enough of it, it could give you a high you wouldn't believe. No such brew as root beer was likely to replace that.

My next encounter with the scent was in a paste soap for washing plaster walls. This drew my attention to the fact that industry seemed to have adopted a modest odor code founded on natural oils, thus:

toothpaste	spearmint	*Mentha spicata*
mouthwash	peppermint	*Mentha piperita*
shoe polish	oil of myrrhbane	*Balsamodendron myrrha*
floor wax	red cedar	*Juniperus virginiana*
liquid floor soap	pine oil	*Pinus palustris*
wall washing paste	sassafras	*Sassafras variifolium*

Of all of these and other aromas and flavors, the most American was sassafras. Columbus was the first European to get a whiff of it. He said he could sense the nearness of land, long before landfall, from the sassafras scent wafting over the water. It was in the South, in Florida, that the Spanish identified this tree that had long been known to the Indians. It was in Florida, too, that early French settlers gave it the name *sassafras*.

∿

Although *Gray's Botany* reports two varieties of sassafras in eastern Asia, the tree is regarded as originally and peculiarly American. It flourishes in the Caribbean, from Florida to Maine, and in Arkansas and Missouri, where some of the most abundant stands occur.

Its growth varies. Certain trees in North Carolina have reached heights of 120 feet. Farther north, on my farm in Pennsylvania, sassafras is no less prolific than it is in the south, but the trees seldom grow taller than twenty to thirty feet.

Sassafras has a curious shape. The limbs incline to be twisted and snakelike. The lower limbs and twigs tend to drop away, concentrating most of the growth and the foliage in a broad layer at the top, like a flattened umbrella. The trees grow along hedgerows and are seldom found in a wood. The young bark is smooth and light green; the older bark, smooth and orange brown. The wood is light, soft, weak, brittle, coarse grained, slightly aromatic and a dull orange brown. Once the wood was used for boat building, cooperage and fencing. It was a poor material for all of these purposes. Once Indians chewed twigs of it to sweeten their breath. For that purpose it was excellent.

The leaves, which begin chartreuse, like the blossoms, then darken, are shaped like mittens. Some have the thumb on the left, some have it on the right, some have three fingers, some two, some only one. Hence, *variifolium*. These leaves turn a beautiful orange scarlet in autumn. The seeds, which develop in August, are quite a sight. They are blue green, about the size of a navy bean and stand upon brilliant crimson stems that look like golf tees.

∿

Long before Europeans arrived in the Americas—there are suggestions of a history going back beyond 2000 B.C.—the Indians had perfected most of the uses of sassafras. The Onondaga Indians had given it a name, *Wah-*

eh-nak-kas, fragrant stick. They taught the uses of sassafras to the early settlers. The strongest oil concentration lay in the bark of the roots, and this, the Indians disclosed, was the part that should be used to make tea.

Sir Francis Drake brought sassafras roots back to Europe in 1586, which suggests that the roots were an item the Indians kept in ready supply. Tea made from these roots, called saloop, promptly became such a rage in England, both as a beverage and as a cure-all, that small street stands set up everywhere to sell it.

Sassafras grew to be the first great crop that the Americas exported to Europe. It was in demand long before tobacco gained its market. Seventeenth-century records show large sassafras shipments from colonial Virginia. The demand for the roots, as both medicine and refresher, was so great in Europe that the hunt for it inspired much early American exploration. Gosnold, for instance, felt his 1602 voyage of discovery was rewarded completely when he found prolific groves of sassafras at Martha's Vineyard. Its popularity produced nicknames: ague tree, saxifrax, cinnamon wood and, imitating the Indians, smelling stick.

The tea is prepared by infusing a teaspoon of crumbled sassafras root bark in a cup of boiling water. Years of experiment and medical thought suggest that the only therapeutic value of sassafras may be a mild ability to reduce fever. Even so, we know enough about the effectiveness of placebos to accept that in an era when people believed drinking sassafras tea could cure many ills, the drinking of it may have generated a variety of psychosomatic miracles.

The sassafras bonanza was done in, as most bonanzas are, by excessive zeal. The very explorers who brought back the joys of sassafras also brought back the cause of its equally sudden disfavor. The Spanish and French imported the dread venereal disease, syphilis. When word got about that sassafras was the remedy the Indians used to cure the French Pox, as it was called, no one cared to be seen drinking the tea in public for fear of being suspected of a shameful secret.

Despite a season of neglect, sassafras's decidedly medicinal aroma attracted new attention. Even if it were not efficacious, it ought to be antiseptic. This may account for its modern popularity as a fragrance for medicines and cleansers. Also, there are still some, the authors of *Herbs and Medicinal Flowers* among them, who do not yield to the medical consensus. They believe sassafras to be a sweet-smelling essential oil that could be used as a stimulant and carminative and say the wood is sudorific (sweat producing, like aspirin).

Medicinal or not, sassafras is still a delightful ingredient of food and drink. Root beer was made from it, and the flavor of root beer is still sassafras. Tea brewed from the bark is a delightful, deep red, aromatic drink that may be as sweet or as dry as the sipper likes. Nelson Coon says, in *Using Wayside Plants*, that by grating the dried bark into boiling sugar, one can make a strongly flavored condiment for meat.

Dr. Pritiken, in a diet that was a great rage in the 1980s, stated that sassafras was a carcinogen. So is the burned part of a steak, if one must be fussy. It seems curious, though, that a substance in wide use for nearly five thousand years among people who lived into their eighties and nineties should never have been considered harmful until Dr. Pritiken announced it. I find I have a lot more confidence in the Indians than I have in Dr. Pritiken.

Those who worry should know, by the way, that neither sassafras nor any of the other aromatics in my list is now derived from plants. All are synthesized, and any carcinogens they might contain are thus the fault of the chemists, not the plants.

Indian medicine men made an early mouthwash by mixing essence of sassafras with salt, bayberry and myrrh. The Choctaw Indians in Louisiana developed filé, a seasoning they taught to the Acadians, who became the Cajuns. Filé has become a staple condiment for Creole cooking and is in enough demand to provide a modest living for those who make it.

These men make filé by gathering and slow-drying young sassafras leaves, pounding them to a powder and pressing the powder through a fine sieve to achieve a talcumlike texture. Filé thickens soup or stew in the same way that okra does. But whereas okra can be cooked in a gumbo from the start, filé cannot be. It must be added at the last minute, else it forms tough threads. These threads seem to have suggested the name, filé, from the French word *filet*, which means thread. So sensitive is this last-minute adding that some Louisiana chefs will not do it in the kitchen. They put shakers of filé on the table so that diners can do their own thickening. Filé, which imparts a delicate flavor, somewhat like a flavor of thyme, must be stored in bottles of colored glass. Sunlight destroys its brilliant green color.

❧

Sassafras grows abundantly in every hedgerow on my Pennsylvania farm. The year I first noticed its spring bonanza, we harvested our first sassafras roots. My sons and I were clearing a part of a pasture where two volunteer sassafras stood. It was spring and the soil was well soaked. When we pulled the trees with our tractor, they came out roots and all. The moment the roots appeared, they filled the air with perfume. We washed the roots, dried them and peeled away their bark.

The roots of two moderate-sized, fifteen-foot trees gave us two quarts of crumbled bark. It looks to me as if enough new trees spring up to allow us to harvest bark from a tree or two each year without depleting the supply. All one needs is one or two sassafras to have abundant seedlings.

If we wished to replenish the home stand, we could transplant from a hedgerow. Helen Van Pelt Wilson says in *The Fragrant Years* that she had complete success transplanting three-foot whips that were in early leaf even though they were missing most of their long taproots.

I have tried to make filé. I think an amateur with more patience than I might manage it. I didn't get enough leaves and the ones I got were too old. Meanwhile the tea is enough. Its fragrance brings back a feel of older times, of front verandas, amateur baseball games, afternoons at fairgrounds and summer evenings at concerts.

Those are lots of rewards from a small and pretty tree.

EDUCATIONAL
ADVENTURES

❧

Lumbering Experience

Few things take up less space than a tree standing; few take more than a tree lying down. Like many other people, I never discovered this until I became the owner of a woodlot, a wood or a forest. All of these are inexact terms for stands of timber. I have sought in vain the breakpoints in numbers of acres at which a woodlot becomes a wood (the singular is correct) or a wood, a forest. The gradation seems to be a vague count of numbers of trees, viz: woodlot = some; wood = many; forest = great many.

We had twenty acres of wood. Fifteen were a part of a forty-acre forest that we shared with our neighbor, Hebe Dick. The other five, at the back of our property, were a part of a thirty-acre forest we shared with a choleric farmer named Funderwite. Our immediate reaction to our wood was that it was beautiful, lovely to look at, doing fine, let it alone.

Probably fifty years had passed since our wood had been lumbered. The stands were chiefly tulip poplar with random oak, ash, cherry, hickory, black walnut and sweet gum plus an abundant sprinkling of silver beech and dogwood. Because most of our trees were mature and large, our wood was pleasantly gloomy at midday, with big trunks, some bent, some straight, like columns in a sylvan temple, raising against the sun a dense canopy of leaves. Mimi and I liked to walk there. It was like wandering in the enchanted forest of Hansel and Gretel.

At noon on still days in spring and summer, the constant gloaming had a mystic stillness that the sudden hammering of a woodpecker would startle, or a bird crying, "Larch, larch, larch!" or another screaming in shrewish tones, "You beast! You beast! You beast, you!" Windy days brought a sound like a great cataract hurling torrents down an abyss. When rains came, even downpours, the wood stayed dry for a long while. When, at last, the water dripped its way down, rain would fall in the wood long after the skies had cleared. Every edge of our wood opened upon a fresh scene. Each was a door to a different theater where a different stage was set.

The winds and snows and ice of winter brought down trees and large branches. We would hear one fall in a distant crash and would peer into the wood, seeking the cause. Our next walk would show us: an uprooted tree, its circle of roots standing like an earth-clogged wheel, punctuated with boulders and stones that the roots had wrenched from the ground.

We did little with these windfalls. We cut some into firewood, but being in the era of cheap central heating with coal or oil, we did this for fun, not need. The windfalls gave us their greatest bonus when they rotted. We dug from the logs buckets of humus the color of cola and the texture of stale bread and brought it to nourish broadleaf evergreens.

It didn't occur to us to cut timber for sale or for any other purpose. We knew, vaguely, that wood was a crop like corn or wheat and that a wood should be harvested at regular intervals. But that kind of wood management seemed to be for those great tracts of forests on mountains that you saw from the windows of trains and never considered as owned by anybody.

A storm, in 1948, gave us an inkling of lumbering. It brought down six trees in our fifteen-acre wood: five poplars and a cherry. This ill wind blew good for a few free-lance lumbermen. One came and offered to buy sawlogs from our downed trees. He didn't want to pay much, but he hauled out a big roll of bills and offered to pay cash on the spot. It looked like found money.

Mimi wanted the cherry sawlog for furniture wood. The lumberman put this log on blocks near the barn. It lay there, twenty feet long, eighteen inches in diameter and weighing about a ton. What Mimi supposed we might do with it, I never learned. I did learn that nobody but a logger with a big truck and a crane can move a sawlog anywhere. Until a sawmill reduces it to planks, a sawlog is of no earthly use.

It is, however, perishable. Left in the open, a log starts rotting at once. Ours needed about five years to rot entirely. Meanwhile, it was a good conversation piece.

∾

Hebe Dick got us into woodcutting. At one of her Sunday dinners we found ourselves in the presence of Reginald Forbes.

Reginald Forbes was tall, classically gray and sinewy with a complexion that sun and wind had etched an Indian red. He wore his chin drawn in. Vertical creases marked his jowls. He was the very model of a civil engineer. His piercing blue eyes penetrated far horizons and conjured up designs for massive structures. His square hands held canapés delicately but gave an impression of restrained but crushing strength. He conversed with Mrs. Dick in capable French.

He had taken his degree in civil engineering, he told us, but actually he was a forester. He examined forests that needed thinning, selected the trees to be cut, marked them, got the owner's approval, found a lumberman to buy the logs, supervised the cutting, collected the money, and paid the owner. This sounded interesting, but we couldn't see how it concerned us until Mrs. Dick, with many a fluting, girlish shriek, dramatized how desperately she needed money to buy a really fine piece of West Virginia property, to which she proposed to move. Our countryside, she said, had had its day and could do nothing now but decline. The only way she could find to get the money was to sell some of her timber. Because we shared a wood—she smiled to show how this made us all cozy and family—she thought we might like to seize the chance to make a little wood money, too.

We were at the stage in our lives when any money was badly needed money. But Mimi hated to think what it would do to her fairy-tale wood.

"I suppose," I said to Forbes, "that, if Mrs. Dick cut wood, the cutters would honor our line."

"More or less." He gave a boys-will-be-boys grin. "A woodsman's view is that he can cut as far across a line as he can throw an axe."

So if we didn't cut, we could lose a good deal of our wood anyhow. Forbes was sympathetic but authoritative. Our wood really did need thinning. He would choose carefully. He would walk our wood with us and cut nothing that we wanted to save. He expected to take no more than a third of our timber. He mainly wanted tulip poplar.

He marked our trees in two places: a large blaze at breast height and a small one on the root. He colored each blaze with red wax. With a special hammer he struck and embedded an F in each blaze. If a lumberman cut an unmarked tree, the missing root blaze would tell on him. Forbes brought a contract signed by a lumberman. When we signed it, he handed us a check for the total payment.

I was working in Philadelphia when the cutting occurred. Mimi told me it was happening, but she wouldn't go and look. When I went back in the dusk that summer evening, all I could see was great looming trucks and trailers of sawlogs. By Saturday the cutting was finished and the men were gone.

We went to look at our wood. What a mess! The lumbermen had taken only the sawlogs. Tops, broken limbs, stumps and brush lay in such tangles that we couldn't walk through any longer. We had to climb through. No trees without the Forbes blazes had been cut, but a lot of unmarked trees had been destroyed because cut trees had fallen on them and shattered them. In our side of the wood alone, it looked like more than a hundred cords of firewood had been left to rot. But the year was 1952. The market for firewood was so poor that a lumberman could not recover the cost of cutting and hauling it.

According to Forbes, trees should be harvested regularly to let sunlight penetrate and stimulate new growth. Some young trees did come up, but what actually got stimulated was briers, poison ivy, Virginia creeper, wineberries, wild grape and sumac. Blazing sunlight destroyed all feel of a dark and ancient fairy-tale forest.

We resolved never to allow cutting again or, if we did, to insist on the removing of the limbs and tops. We did have to allow it. By 1959, Mrs. Dick had bought up most of a county in West Virginia and was preparing to sell out and move. She wanted to glean income from a last cutting. This time we held the cutting to a minimum. We dealt directly with the lumberman. He couldn't afford to cut and take the firewood, but he could rough-cut the slash and stack it. It was some help. We managed to bring out most of the firewood.

∾

Although you can have lumbermen or refuse to have them, you can't refuse to have storms. A severe storm in the 1960s dropped five of our trees across our fence line and onto the land of Funderwite, the farmer. He informed us of this in harsh terms and ordered us to get our trees off his property without damaging his clover crop, onto which they had fallen. I think if a farmer owned the Sahara desert and a neighbor's palm tree fell on it, it would turn out to have been a clover crop.

Funderwite had a reputation for attacking people with a manure fork, a lethal tool with four sharp tines. Also, trees that fell across property lines could produce complicated legal questions. If the person onto whose property they fell tampered with the trees, he might get sued to recover their value. If their falling had damaged the neighbor's fencing or anything else, the owner of the trees must use the proceeds of any sale to repair the damage. Or so it was explained to us.

We had come to know a tough old woodsman named Ed Ray. We put the problem into his hands.

He met Funderwite at the trees and pointed out that a stretch of hardscrabble with a few wisps of greenbrier was hardly a clover field. Funderwite stabbed at the ground with the manure fork. He was dangerous with a fork, he said. Ed Ray fingered the edge of his axe, which flashed angry

71

flecks of sunlight. He was pretty handy with an axe, he said. That settled everything.

In exchange for the sawlogs, Ray cut all of the firewood. I'd never before seen such a man with an axe. He stood for hours and split great boles as comfortably as a cook slicing cucumbers. He brought the wood to our barn. When I got it stacked, it came to ten cords.

More recently we have found that wood can be harvested cleanly, without damage and with considerable profit. What you need is a woodsman who does not consider lumbering a form of strip mining. The one who found us was a local Latvian named Gus Jermacans, a great, red-headed Paul Bunyan of a man with the joyous outlook of the Ghost of Christmas Present. Gus cut neatly and tidily, piled all slash in designated places and replanted all haul roads with grass. He paid about four times the rate we had gotten earlier. Two years after he left, the only way you would know the place had been lumbered was by the stacks of slash not yet cut for firewood and somewhat more sunlight in the wood.

How to Roast a Log

It is curious how intensely living in the country focuses attention on trees. Trees surround and enclose farms; standing in ranks, living guardians, they govern weather and comfort, diffuse harsh winds, control drifting snow, supply fruits and nuts and, when they fall, provide firewood.

The practices of heating houses with wood have made two complete cycles in fewer than a hundred years: from fireplaces to stoves to fireplaces to stoves. I have participated in one and a half of these cycles, having begun with no knowledge at all of fire making.

I suppose that any ancient who did not learn to start fires died of starvation and failed to evolve into civilized man. The Neanderthal who did survive probably could whip up a cave fire with a twist of a stick or a spark from a rock and keep a steady blaze encouraged with drippings from broiling mammoth steaks.

I, however, had had this knack bred out of me. I grew up in Atlanta, where fireplaces weren't needed. Forsaken in a wilderness, I would have perished as soon as the season changed and the raw nuts and berries ran out. Not until I moved to our farm was I confronted with such urgencies as fireplaces and woodstoves. Or, rather, was I confronted with the residual evidences of woodstoves in front of boarded-up fireplaces.

The practical farm family who lived in our house before us had discovered the defect of the fireplace. A fireplace sucks up more warm air than it puts out. So the farm family closed the fireplaces and installed potbellied stoves. From these, pipes rose through the ceiling to the room above and, if needed, through a second ceiling to the room above that before entering the chimney. These stoves and their ascending pipes got a house warm and kept it warm. They were ugly, of course. Perfect frights. They added no grace to milady's boudoir, but they guaranteed her a warm boudoir.

Before we took over, the world had learned about central heating, and the farm family had put in an early version. The only remaining evidences of stoves were pipe holes in floors and ceilings and charred spots on floors where stoves had spit hot coals. Fuel for central heating was so cheap that keeping warm would never again be a problem. One could even afford to use a fireplace! Why worry about losing a little heat? So, joining the other modern buyers of farmhouses, we opened a fireplace.

But not immediately. The coal furnace installed by the farm family blew hot air through a single huge register in the living room. A vent in the ceiling led to the room above, giving us one warm bedroom. The rest of the house got heated by any warmth that managed to drift into it. Our cookstove was a coal range. Our water heater was a bucket-a-day stove. It was supposed to produce an endless supply of hot water from a bucket a day of coal. It produced a bucket a day of hot water from an endless supply of coal. Mimi, raised in the country, managed the coal range with fair efficiency. She never mastered the bucket-a-day. She could produce two products with it: ice water or superheated steam. Ours was the only toilet I ever saw boil.

So our first money expenditures went into an electric water heater and an electric range. Not until we got those did we feel we had entered the twentieth century. A year later, we installed an oil furnace to produce hot-air heat. Now we could finally open our fireplace.

Before we had moved from the city, we had watched a friend, Bill Dall, who had grown up in Boston, operate a fireplace. His fires, which he nourished with an occasional chunk of wood, were tidy as tea parties. I was impressed by Bill's fires and longed to imitate him.

Our own operable fireplace had been closed with some large and efficient wooden doors. Behind these lay a cavern. Great winds swept through it, blowing down soot and the feathers of starlings, sucking out the heat from the house along with bits of paper and light objects. Here, the original farmer cooked, snugly surrounded by his family. How lovely it would be to reenact this charming scene. All I had to do was light a few logs, the way I supposed Bill Dall did, and watch them burn.

How easy that sounded. And to Bill Dall, how easy it was. But not for me. I had always believed the way you set fire to large logs was with a few newspapers. To those who don't know better, let me say that you can't. You might as well try to light a steel beam with a safety match. Burn upward of a bale of newspapers under logs and you will do little more than char them.

I tried it. The charred logs produced smoke without heat. The smoke had a delightfully woodsy fragrance that enchanted me for fully five minutes. Then it gagged me. I opened doors and windows, letting smoke out and cold in. This taught me it was far better to be cold without smoke than with it.

My charred logs were self-stimulating. They never burned, they never actually went out. They just lay there belching smoke. I tried to put them out by sprinkling them with water. The result was steam as well as smoke. This taught me another farm truth: a room that is already cold and smoky does not need humidity.

∾

I learned to use kindling. It was better, but it didn't always work. Often it caught beautifully, making a friendly crackling and some heat, but producing only smoke above the logs. No good. Smoke on top, at the sides, in fact, smoke in any quantity anywhere in the fireplace was, in three minutes, a smoky room; in five, a smoky house.

Now and then, when the wind was right, I did manage to set fire to a log or two, but chiefly I produced smoke and smoking logs. I soon realized it was my lot not to burn logs but to roast them over fires made of kindling. If, in my house, you saw what you supposed was the blazing fire of song and story where logs burned cheerily, you would have been wrong. What you would have been looking at was a room kept sort of warm by burning kindling over which logs were roasting.

During this part of my education, I neglected another precaution that all beginners should learn. Never burn rotting wood in a fireplace. One frosty Saturday I found several large sections of fallen apple tree. We were short of logs handy to the house, and I had often heard praise for the fragrance of burning apple wood. As I sawed the tree to lengths, I was pleased to note, that, being rotten, it cut like butter. A few insects and worms rolled out of the cuts and perished in the freezing air. I built my fire, lit it and leaned back to savor apple smoke. As the kindling burned brightly, more insects squirmed out of weevil holes and dropped sizzling into the flames.

The kindling burned out, smoldered and died. The logs went on smoking. The room filled with smoke. Then it filled with insect life. The heat of the kindling had alarmed and galvanized the borers, the weevils, the nits and gnats, the flies, the ants and the termites. Those logs must have had a population in the millions, and every individual there thought summer had come.

Hunting down the legions of ants, flies, beetles and weevils took three days. Weeks later we would find the odd borer, wandering around the house in a lost, bemused way, wondering how came a heat wave in the midst of a hard frost.

❧

By the time I learned to start a fire with a teacup of kerosene, fuel oil had grown so cheap that we used our fireplace only for show. We had been lulled into a false sense of security.

Hurricane Hazel, in October 1954, brought our first jarring awakening. The eye of this hurricane passed within thirty miles of our farm. Admittedly, it was a freak. We were more than a hundred miles from a shore that hurricanes tended only to graze.

The wind began at five in the afternoon, reached gale force by seven and blew until nearly midnight. It blew shingles from roofs and pushed down trees. Our stone house was so solid that, with the doors closed, we heard little wind and felt none. We could pretend that there was no storm. Until nine o'clock. At nine o'clock, the power went off and the house began to cool.

The next morning was crisp, crystal clear and a mess. Shingles from the barn roof lay scattered over our lawn like playing cards. Fallen trees crisscrossed the road like jackstraws. Our power and telephone lines stretched beneath them, taut as banjo strings. The power lines were broken. Miraculously, the telephone lines were not.

No electricity meant no heat, no light, no stove, no water. After two days, the novelty of being pioneers, cooking over an open fire, hauling water and living by the light of candles and kerosene lamps paled. All of our cookware grew sooty and greasy. The only water to wash it, or anything else, had to be brought in bottles from our springhouse and heated on the fire. Our beds were cold and dank. We were astonished to see how quickly a house without power became a slum. At the end of eight days, our house looked like some outpost on Hudson Bay. When, on the eighth night, the lights suddenly blazed on, the oil furnace rumbled into action and the pump pushed water through our plumbing, we stared at each other like startled owls.

Relief, I suppose, cures caution. We comforted ourselves with the thought that, where we lived, being struck by a major hurricane couldn't happen often. Then came the blizzard of March 1959.

If this snow had been cold and dry, we would have had a monumental plowing problem, for nearly thirty inches of snow fell, but otherwise, we would have been snug. Instead, the snow was wet and freezing. Ice accumulated on wires and trees and brought everything down. There were places where wires, telephone poles, vines and trees looked as if they had been scrambled in a blender. This time we had no power for ten days.

We finally got the message. If you live in the country, you can never be free of the need to burn wood. When we added our wing, the year after the blizzard, instead of having a new fireplace in our main room downstairs, Mimi insisted on an outlet for a stove. She found a Hudson

River Valley cast-iron stove, shaped like a castle with molded shingles and iron roses, and installed it. The next power shortage, only a day long, we lit it. What joy! No smoke, no weevils, no drafts drawing heat up the chimney. Just plenty of warmth. With a place on top to cook, we had no more burned pans or sooty utensils.

Mimi liked this stove so well that she bought a second, smaller one and put it into one of our previously sealed flues. As if repulsed, now power outages seldom lasted more than an hour or two, so our stoves became pets. We called the larger Ermengarde, the smaller, Clothilde, and we burned them as a stunt for parties.

Who could imagine that the cost of a gallon of fuel oil could soar from about 20 cents to more than a $1.30? As oil prices took off on this giddy flight, we began to burn our stoves every night.

❧

Alas, Ermengarde and Clothilde were not equal to the incessant burning needed to combat a fuel-oil shortage. We were swept up in the national panic of 1979–1980, when everyone feared that reasonably priced fuel oil was gone forever. Our annual oil bill soared from an average of $1,200 to an average of $2,300. It was time for drastic action.

With a twenty-acre wood, we had no shortage of fuel, but we needed a safe way to burn it. The stove market was booming. Stove outlets and chimney sweeps popped up everywhere. Stoves from France and the Scandinavian and Slavic countries dominated the market. These countries had never stopped heating with wood. They had developed a range of stoves that were brilliantly colored and shaped like barbarian altars or ancient mangles. The object of these designs was to travel the smoke through mazes of baffles before releasing it—its heat squeezed out—into a chimney. Such a stove was 85 percent efficient compared with 35 percent for Ermengarde and Clothilde, 10 percent for the fireplace.

We bought a small French stove to replace Clothilde. It was a pretty thing. It didn't look so much like a stove as a piece of ornate pastry with lots of whipped cream. It issued more heat than Clothilde, but being designed to burn coal, it seldom held a wood fire overnight. The next year we replaced Ermengarde with something really authoritative. We bought an American soapstone stove. It was and is a delight. It may lose more heat up the chimney, but it generates less creosote. Fed any kind of decent wood, it seldom goes out unless we deprive it of fuel for about eighteen hours.

When the price of oil went back down to 70 cents a gallon, we didn't burn the stoves so much. We hadn't the incentive to lay in full supplies of wood for a winter. We chiefly burned windfalls. Cutting and hauling these gave us pleasant afternoons of exercise. But now that we have the stoves, we don't see ever totally stopping.

A man in the country is atavistically committed to wood. His predecessors burned it. He also has a kind of obligation. Downed timber is a by-product of owning a wood. If one doesn't convert it to firewood and burn it indoors, one must occasionally make great pyres of it outdoors— an atrocious waste of heat energy.

Always, too, there is the possibility of long power outages. Wherever power lines run on poles above ground, they are vulnerable to high winds, heavy wet snows and the devastations of out-of-control vehicles, trains and aircraft. When such outages occur, the household that can keep warm and do a bit of nonsmoky cooking can endure a good deal of living by romantic candlelight.

Finally, there is no guarantee that international cupidity and world politics may not produce another oil shortage, or that an enemy attack may not sever our electrical or oil umbilical cord. It may seem absurd to make Noah's Ark–type preparations for unlikely catastrophes, but one of the joys of living in the country is that you have the space and the time to take such precautions.

In the face of the unlikely catastrophe, we will be glad to have our stoves and our wood supplies. But not our fireplaces. For us a fireplace is just a place to roast a log.

A Home-Grown Chop

Close behind the urge to supply one's own heat is the urge to supply one's own food. The usual first step is a truck garden that yields gluts of some vegetables and none of others. However that works out, one quickly appreciates that the real place to save food money is on meat.

Having reached that understanding, it is a short step to deciding to raise chickens. Fenced into a reasonably large pen and given auxiliary feed, chickens will supply both eggs and meat.

Being contrary, however, and impinged upon by other influences, we didn't go that way. Our first foray into meat was raising sheep. We had lots of pasture deeply overgrown with everything, including murderous brier. We thought sheep could solve two problems: clean up the pasture and supply meat. They did clean up the pasture, but we couldn't eat any of our sheep. They all had names. We knew them personally. We had stayed up all night during lambing to assist deliveries. We had bottle-fed lambs that ewes abandoned—usually the third lamb of triplets—and docked all tails and castrated the young rams.

We had to seek our meat elsewhere. We had bought a thirty-cubic-foot freezer to house our provender. And what was it storing now? Two loaves of bread and a packet of garlic.

All of this was right after World War II, a conflict during which meat had been rationed and most decent cuts had become unobtainable. Playing on four years of yearning appetites, merchants everywhere urged the purchase of whole animals, steers on the hoof, halves or quarters to be butchered to taste, and the services of rental lockers for storing frozen meat in carcass-size quantities. We were tempted by all of this, but in 1948, the initial investment for a steer, 30 cents per pound for a thousand pounds of live weight, was beyond our budget and our needs.

Mimi, fascinated by the bulk meat idea, pondered an alternative to a steer and came up with a hog. It seemed a good compromise. I had been raised in the South, where pork was much more prevalent than beef. The attraction of having our own bacon, ham and fresh pork shoulder was irresistible. Most attractive was having decent sausage.

Southern pork sausage was not considered choice unless it was pure pork, tremendously hot and full of sage. It should be hot enough to make you sweat under the eyes. For years, I had tried every brand of mid-Atlantic fresh pork sausage I could find. All were flat, tame stuff with the texture of baked mush and a mild flavor of nutmeg. The only thing flatter and more flavorless was the British link sausage called a banger. But with our own hog we could have real sausage.

Mimi bought a two-hundred-pound hog and sent it to a local butcher. When I told the butcher the proportions of pepper and sage I wanted in my sausage, he said I was crazy.

Finally, I was going to get plenty of sausage flavored to my taste. I got plenty, all right. We got forty pounds. We also got two ten-pound hams, two five-pound flitches of bacon, two seven-pound pork shoulders, and twenty pounds of pork chops, plus thirty-five pounds of scrapple and thirty pounds of lard.

No matter how you feel about scrapple, thirty-five pounds of it is too much by thirty pounds. We ate some, gave away as much as we could and fed the rest to the dogs.

The lard was more difficult. Thirty pounds of lard is an impressive sight. It is a lovely creamy color, it has a rich, nutty aroma and it will fill a washtub.

Many a fine pastry recipe makes much of the excellence of pork lard as a shortening. Until you have had a piecrust made with pork lard, say they, you have never known piecrust. Until you have eaten doughnuts fried in deep pork fat, you don't know what doughnuts can be.

All well and good. But thirty pounds of lard must be enough to supply a small village with piecrust and doughnuts. And the trouble with pork lard is that it won't keep. It goes rancid, and it goes pretty rapidly. We had used no more than a pound of ours before it began to stink. I wasn't too concerned. I had majored in chemistry. I knew that the rancid odor was produced by butyric acid, which was volatile and would boil off. I boiled the second pound we used. The lard came out sweet and tasty; the neighborhood came out terrible. Mimi said that that was the last time I would do that. So we had to throw out the remaining lard.

The pork chops were thick and fine. I can't fault those. The pork shoulders were delicious. So was the sausage. For a while. We found, though, that even highly seasoned sausage—or any other ground meat— has a distinctly limited shelf life in a freezer. It didn't spoil. It went flat. A kind of blah flavor replaced the sweet savor of the meat. Even hot pepper and sage couldn't conceal the change.

Because we didn't know how to cure the flitches properly and hadn't the equipment to do it, our bacon was average to poor and the hams were inedible.

I won't give actual prices. Prices then were unusually low; prices today are absurdly high. But I figure the price per pound for the parts of the pig we could use came to about three times the price of the same items in a store.

∾

I did not conclude from my pork experience that buying meat on the hoof was a bad idea. I concluded that we had bought the wrong animal. The animal to try was a steer. By now we could afford one, and we had a son to help eat it. Our steer weighed a thousand pounds on the hoof. The market price was 32 cents per pound. We saved $40 by finding a man who would sell his steer for 28 cents. He had no way to haul the steer to the slaughterer. It took us a week to find a furniture mover who would handle the job for $50.

For butchering, we went back to the butcher who had done our pig. He would go to the slaughterer and pick up the carcass. He asked in which of several ways we wanted our steer subdivided. All we knew was that we wanted two-inch-thick steaks like those served in fancy, expensive restaurants. So we asked him to cut all steaks two inches thick. Keep the rib roasts small—three-rib roasts—but give us as many of those as possible. That ought to do it. Shouldn't it?

Not quite, said our butcher. There was a lot more to consider about the meat of a whole steer than steaks, rib roasts and hamburgers. There were great uncharted acreages of chuck, flank, shoulder, loins, rump, kidneys, heart, liver and tongue. What had we in mind about these items? Wouldn't we like him to butcher and wrap and mark everything? Anybody we asked about this said: "For goodness' sake, yes! Let him cut and wrap." He would do it for only 11 cents a pound. How many pounds would it be? Between five hundred and six hundred.

To save between $55 and $66, we thought we could handle the rest of the cutting and all of the wrapping and marking. "Well," we said, "give us the rest of the steer as it comes."

"As it comes?"

"Well. Bust up the bones a little bit. We'll decide the shapes and sizes when we see them."

ॐ

The way to get an education is to take wild chances with things you don't understand. Until we got that beef, I thought thirty pounds of pork lard was an arresting sight. Now I know the truth. A butchered whole moose or bison may dress out bigger, but a rough-butchered steer is awesome.

Five days after our steer went to the slaughterer on the hoof, it came away from the butcher in boxes. He called and told us to come and get it. What he bestowed on us were eight large, corrugated packing cases, each holding seventy pounds of beef.

The weather being warmish, Mimi and I knew that if we didn't get the whole business cut, wrapped and frozen as quickly as possible, we would have a charnel house on our hands.

We tackled the steaks first. The sirloins, clubs, T-bones and porterhouses were easy to deal with. Being thick, each looked like a small roast, but each at least had finite limits. The steak that rocked us was the beef equivalent of a hamsteak. Such steaks from a steer measured nearly a yard the long way, a foot and a half the narrow way and, being two inches thick, each weighed eight to ten pounds. There were fourteen of these to each side. Even cut into thirds, one steak could serve about six people.

The hamburger came in three large drums: eighty pounds of it, which had to be wrapped in one-pound packages. The liver came in two big lumps. There was thirty pounds of liver. We knew it should be sliced and we went at it courageously. Slicing liver compares to slicing a bucket of blackberry Jell-O. But we had asked for the liver as it came. That was how it came.

The way liver came was nowhere near so appalling as the way the rest of the animal came. It came in boulders of beef the size of kettledrums and was absolutely unidentifiable. We got out large color charts we'd collected, charts purporting to show the various cuts of beef as they ought to look. The cuts in the pictures were neat and clean, clearly recognizable from the way the bones and fat ran. Our massive chunks of beef bore no resemblance to anything in these pictures. They were covered with blood and gore and leaked constantly. There was nothing for it but to slice ad lib. Anything left over would be soup bones.

Working full time as fast as we could, it took us eighteen hours a day for two days to get the steer cut, wrapped and frozen. Our two setters attended the ceremony. They were keenly interested for the first half day. It seemed stingy not to let them enjoy our glut of beef. So we kept tossing them tasty trimmings. By afternoon, they were so bored with beef, they wouldn't even come into the kitchen, where we worked.

Once our job was done, we felt rich. With all that beef we had only to buy potatoes. We gorged on steaks and hamburgers. Presently we worked down to a freezer full of roasts and soupbones. Because neither of us liked liver, kidneys or tongue, we gave those away. By entertaining a little more than usual, we worked our way through the roasts until, increasingly, the package we took to be a small roast turned out to be a large soupbone. At last, to clear out the freezer, we converted the soupbones to bouillon.

How did we come out? If we figured all of the costs against the weight of the meat we used, omitting the weight of livers, kidneys, and tongue or soupbones, our hamburger cost us 10 to 15 percent above market, our roasts were about right and our steaks were maybe 10 percent below market. On average, we paid the same prices we would have paid to a store.

When more children came along, three boys in all, and we could use an entire steer every nine months, buying steers paid. But we never again took on cutting and wrapping.

∾

By the time we got our steer purchases organized, it seemed time to try to do something with our sheep. In four years our flock had grown to forty-some ewes and a ram, and we no longer knew them. Naturally we culled the poorest-looking ewes for slaughter, and naturally, we were disappointed with the yield. The proportion of bones to meat in a sheep seemed to me the highest in any animal. Probably that was why lamb was always so expensive. From one of our sheep we were lucky to get enough meat to make a decent Irish stew.

We could have done better by selecting our best ewes and docked rams, penning them up and pouring corn and other feed into them for sixty days, then slaughtering them. Had we been doing nothing but farming and trying to subsist on our produce, we might have handled our sheep this way. For us, the additional work and expense would not have yielded enough rewards.

Our irascible and hostile neighbor, Farmer Funderwite, got us out of the sheep business. Our flock had kept growing. Sheep foraged everywhere. Finally they broke through into the lands of the testy Funderwite, whose miserable crop—it was alfalfa this time—was waiting to be damaged.

Funderwite called. My sheep had broken into his alfalfa field and eaten half of it.

"I got 'um penned up in my barn. Forty of 'um. You want 'um back"— he savored every word—"gonna cost you ten dollars a sheep. Ten dollars, you come right now and get 'um. 'Cause I'm leaving tonight for a trip."

I could almost hear his mind at work. My sheep were going to pay for his trip with money left over.

"I'm giving you a break," he said. "Big break. That alfalfa was worth more'n four hundred dollars. You wait and they gonna cost you fifteen apiece plus grain while I'm gone."

The value of forty cadaverous sheep was $600? Ridiculous! I knew and he knew that anybody who would pay even $5 each for those scrawny animals would be crazy. Still, they had value. He would feed them for market. The poor beasts needed that break. I let silence creep in and stretch out. Then I said:

"What sheep? I haven't lost any sheep."

Quietly, before he could say a word, I hung up.

Chasing Wild Mushrooms

Europeans have always been enthusiastically venturesome about wild mushrooms. Americans, after the first generation, have not been. Perhaps the long availability of *Agaricus campestris*, the field or meadow mushroom, both fresh and canned in large quantities and at low prices has made us lazy. Lazy enough to lose our curiosity, our interest and our cunning about the natural treasures.

Agaricus campestris is said to be fairly easy to identify, when found in the wild, and reasonably foolproof, if simple precautions are observed. Too often, though, people gathering wild field mushrooms have poisoned themselves by mixing in specimens of amanitas, most frequently *Amanita verna*, the destroying angel. These mushrooms are so poisonous that just carrying one or two of them, mixed with safe mushrooms, can produce lethal results. Fear of this has deterred general interest in wild mushrooms. Propose to most people that you intend to gather and cook wild mushrooms and they will react as if you had said you were going to hurl yourself from a high roof or pop half a dozen strychnine tablets.

Mimi and I were no exceptions. With sixty-five acres of woods and fields teeming with delicious food, there for the picking, we hewed to custom. We stuck to commercial mushrooms. When we walked our property, we trod down morels, kicked away puffballs and demolished oyster mushrooms as if we were ridding the world of objects foul and fetid.

One year, after a herd of cows spent the summer in our front pasture, the autumn rains brought up puffballs thick as pumpkins in a patch. Angelo Sparano, the Italian mason who built our ha-ha wall, drove by and saw them. Could he and his wife pick them? Sure. We watched, shaking our heads. They picked and took away three bushels of puffballs.

༼ఴ༽

Little reliable literature about American mushrooms was available before 1960. Most of the earlier books had been printed in Europe for the European market. Although those books offered some guidance, most of the European varieties looked different from their American counterparts. Had the literature stayed that way, we might never have enjoyed our mushroom abundance.

But early in the sixties the University of Michigan Press published Alexander H. Smith's superb *Mushroom Hunter's Field Guide*. This was the first book we had seen that described and codified American wild mushrooms, of which there must be nearly a thousand varieties. Smith, a man who clearly did his own field work and gloried in it, took a swashbuckling approach to gathering and eating. Some mushrooms, he remarked casually, were poisonous to one person, edible to another. Some, though edible or, at any rate, not poisonous—the shelf mushrooms, for instance, that appeared in layers on trees—were objectionably tough. Some were edible so long as not ingested with alcohol. It was a personal log and a delight. Unfortunately, the illustrations were in black and white. This was a drawback. Color has a lot to do with identifying wild mushrooms. Finally, the mushrooms Smith described were from the middle and western states. Identical species in the east would often vary from western ones in shape, size and color.

Even so, his guide to the morchellae, the morels, convinced us that no poisonous mushroom resembled the true morels. This is almost accurate.

There are false morels and, of the two of these reported as poisonous in the Roger Tory Peterson field guide to North American mushrooms, the *Gyromitra esculenta* does look somewhat like the true morel. Instead of being aggressively phallic in shape, however, it is squashed down, flattened and not likely to be confused with edible varieties.

Armed with Smith's knowledge, Mimi and I went into our woods on a Mother's Day weekend, the best time to seek morels. The mayapples had begun to bloom.

We had beginner's luck. We found abundant quantities of *Morchella angusticeps* and M. *esculenta* among mayapples in our beech wood. These mushrooms, always phallic, rose on thick stalks of dead white, cream, yellow and yellowish gray. The heads had vertical spongelike slots and varied in color from russets through shades of orange and yellow to gray.

On our first try, Mimi and I brought home three gallons of morels. We found them more flavorful and much richer than the commercial mushroom, and we appreciated why the morel was considered one of the world's four great delicacies, along with *fraise des bois*, wild strawberries; beluga caviar; and *pâté de fois gras*, goose liver. Sautéed in butter, the morels had a rich, slightly bacon taste. We ate quantities that way, had them with steak and had them in omelets. In later years we learned that morels could be dried and that the dried ones, restored by soaking in water, tasted pretty nearly like the fresh mushroom. Our first pickings never lasted long enough to raise any question of keeping except how long they would keep in the refrigerator.

So far no one knows how to cultivate a morel any more than they know how to cultivate that other mushroom prize, the truffle. The growth of morels, like the growth of most other mushrooms, depends more upon the weather than the growth of almost any other crop. Ideal mushroom weather is cool nights and warm, humid days with a good deal of rain. You don't have to go into the woods to discover whether the weather is right. When the small fairy rings of gray mushrooms spring up in the lawn and volunteer mushrooms of all kinds appear in hedgerows and gardens, mushroom weather has come. When these conditions prevail around the Mother's Day weekend, morel gathering should be good.

After our first bonanza year, though, we went through years of skimpy picking and assumed it was because we had missed the right weekend or the morels had moved from the places where we had last found them. Morels do that. On a rental property we owned, someone had burned a small shed. Where the shed had been, we found a good quantity of Burn-site morels, *Morchella atromentosa*, which have dark, brownish gray caps and rather short stems. Another year, in our wood, we found thick-footed morels, *M. crassipes*, which were two feet tall and three inches in diameter. The three of these in our first find supplied enough morel for eight people to have with steak for dinner.

As one grows older, and the eyesight loses acuteness, one becomes less skillful as a morel hunter. This mushroom's colors and shapes provide a nearly perfect camouflage amidst dried leaves, weathered stones, bark fragments and withered flowers. Today, we send our children and grandchildren on the morel expeditions. They find that, in the proper weather, there is always one part of the wood with morels.

❧

Once started on wild mushrooms, we yearned for more experience and fresh instruction. It was curious that we didn't turn to the boletes and the chanterelles. Although chanterelles were scarcer in our area than elsewhere in the country, we constantly saw boletes. They were easily recognized. Their distinguishing feature was that instead of having gill slits that looked like louvers, they had round holes—hundreds of them—so they looked like a fine-textured sponge. We were constantly kicking these over, but usually at a time when we were busy doing something else. We excused our lack of interest by telling ourselves that we couldn't tell how old these boletes were. Also, while there were many edible boletes, there were many poisonous or dubious ones. Learning about boletes seemed to require more time and study than we could spare.

Finding the small volume *Common Edible Mushrooms* by Clyde M. Christensen stimulated our next hunt. This book had color plates and instructed us on making spore prints, an essential step in identifying mushrooms.

Armed with this book, I toured our wood and found an abundance of a white, soft mushroom growing out of stumps. The mushroom grew in clusters, had a slick, grayish white top and, from beneath, looked like the groined arches in a cathedral. It fitted precisely Christensen's description of *Pleurotus ostreatus*, the oyster mushroom. I ran a spore print to be sure.

For a spore print, you need two pieces of paper, one white, the other black. You place the mushroom cap half on the white paper and half on the black, cover it and allow it to stand until the spore deposits. The spore of my find was white, as it was supposed to be, and showed dramatically on the black paper.

This was when we established our method of sampling. Mimi, not entirely convinced that I had identified my oyster correctly, thought only one of us should venture to eat it. The other should be handy to call an ambulance and explain what had happened. So I sautéed my oyster mushroom, ate it and waited for convulsions.

I survived, and we had a new delight. The oyster mushroom is highly aromatic with an almost cloyingly sweet perfume. Once you have sniffed this scent, you will never forget it. It provides a clue for identifying the oyster quickly. Because you can tire of it, the fragrance is a drawback, but cooking can overcome it.

Oysters are large and, when found, abundant. A single clump can be large enough to yield a three-gallon pail of mushrooms. A week or ten days after one clump is gathered, if the weather continues wet, its stump will have produced another clump. The mushroom will continue to grow on the same stump for several years. The French are said to have favorite oyster-producing stumps that they water regularly to produce continuous crops. The Germans have learned to cultivate this mushroom on fresh-cut stumps in the forest. And just lately the industry has begun to raise and market them commercially, along with shiitakes.

The beauty of the oyster mushroom is that it appears from spring until fall, usually is highly visible and exceptionally plentiful, is lovely cooked and goes with everything. Sliced in long strips and sautéed, the oyster looks like breast of chicken. Lightly sautéed, it retains its fragrance; sautéed until it begins to turn a biscuit color, it loses its apparently volatile fragrance. Then it tastes like nuts.

∾

Having succeeded in these two ventures, we unhesitatingly gathered giant puffballs, *Calvatia gigantea*, and vase puffballs, *C. cyathiformis*, whenever we found them. Puffballs grow in fields where animal manure is abundant. These round or vase-shaped mushrooms hook to the ground through an umbilicus. They have no spore slots. When the spores mature, the ball bursts and scatters them into the wind. Because immature, small puffballs can be confused with amanitas, prudence dictates gathering only large ones. A puffball an inch or two in diameter is a small one. Large ones measure from three inches to more than a foot. We found the best ones to be five to six inches in diameter.

New puffballs are pure white inside with a flesh the consistency of a marshmallow. As the puffball ages, its flesh discolors to yellow, then to an olive green. Although I can find no guidance about eating yellow or green flesh, I have always taken the view that any flesh less than pure white will be inedible, but I may be wrong. The puffball, sort of the beefsteak tomato of the mushrooms, is delicious when sliced to the thickness of scalloped potatoes, sautéed with butter or meat essence and served with meat.

At the peak of our enthusiasm, Mimi found and identified two additional mushrooms, one of which was disappointing, the other of which was the best we ever located, but which we lost.

The disappointing one was a shaggymane, *Coprinus comatus*, one of the inky caps. These, esteemed highly by the English, must be picked and cooked at once. Let stand, they self-digest into a revolting inky fluid. Hence their name.

Mimi found the inky caps first. They grow in fields and have bullet-shaped caps that are shaggy, as if they had been nicked with a razor. Usually they are white with gray gill slits. Mimi saw some in a field about half a mile from our farm and deliberately didn't pick them until I got home. We went together, gathered them and had them cooked within twenty minutes. They tasted like sautéed chalk.

Evidently we did it wrong. When I wrote the above description and published it, a Mr. Francis Cabot of New York City sent proper instructions: pick only those *Coprinus* whose caps are completely attached to the mushroom stems—in short, those that have just emerged above ground and haven't opened. These, he says, will keep until the next mealtime and needn't be rushed into the pot. Blanch the caps briefly by plunging them in boiling water. This stops the inky business and preserves the white color. Finally, rather than sautéing them, poach them gently in simmering butter.

Our delightful find was the *Clitopilus abortivus*, which has no common name. This one showed up in our lawn under the large black walnut. Its cap is usually malformed, hence *abortivus*, because a mold attacks it and destroys a portion. This doesn't hurt its edibility. Mimi found this mushroom and identified it by its pink spore print and white flesh. Our guides suggested that the cap color would be pink, but the ones Mimi found were more often a sort of liverish purple.

Sautéed, this fungus had a nutty mushroom flavor touched with a suggestion of anchovy. It was wonderful and went with everything. By being careful with our mowing in late September and early October, we had abundant crops of these mushrooms, which kept coming for a week or ten days.

I believe the condition of the black walnut under which they were growing governed their growth. The tree was dying, and the *abortivus* appeared only during its last years. Presently, to keep it from falling on the house, we had the tree cut. The *abortivus* disappeared.

The Riches of the Fields

The earth abounds with plenty, if one learns where to seek it. During the 1960s such naturalists as Euell Gibbons issued guides to what could be found: young poke shoots, for instance, as a substitute for asparagus, and dandelion leaves as a substitute for endive in early spring salads. Nature even provided antidotes for her own poisons. Jewelweed, the antidote for poison ivy, usually grew near the ivy.

Mimi and I might have followed Gibbons, when first he blazed across the firmament, but other things distracted us. Our method was to let our goodies press themselves upon us ere we were aware, to insinuate themselves upon our consciousness. As a result, we came upon our treasures in hectic disorder.

The first herb we noticed was tansy, a substitute for sage, nutmeg or cinnamon. A great volunteer patch of *Tanacetum vulgare* grew beside the lane at the creek. We noted the odor and picked a little but did nothing further with it. We were soon growing sage, itself, and nutmeg and cinnamon were available at all stores. Presently a cutter bar, clearing the sides of our lane, mowed down our tansy. Years later, we replanted it in another place.

We discovered pennyroyal, or horsemint, by walking in our fields and pastures. From time to time we would trudge through a patch of weeds that promptly suffused the air with a fragrance like shoe polish. That was our native pennyroyal, *Hedeoma pulegioides*. As we knew of no use for pennyroyal, we didn't pursue that any further.

When we trod on peppermint, *Mentha piperita*, and spearmint, M. *spicata*, we woke up and paid attention. We wasted no time in transplanting clumps close to the house. Neither likes very good soil. Newly cleared hardpan will do. Our soil wasn't quite that bad, but it wasn't great. So our mint beds prospered and allowed us to make lots of mint juleps. The mint julep, according to the instruction I received at my father's knee, is a gentleman's excuse for drinking four ounces of hundred-proof bourbon out of one glass.

At the outset, those were the only herbs that caught our noses and eyes. We were more interested in fruits and nuts.

Our fields had not been planted for two years, and they were rife with wild strawberries, *fraises des bois*. I never learned whether our wild strawberries were the native plant or escaped cultivated berries. So much of our horticulture is escaped, it's hard to judge.

Our largest wild strawberries were not much larger than hickory nuts. Most were the size of navy beans. To pick a pint you had to get on your hands and knees and rummage through a good stretch of weeds, but our twenty acres of open fields were so full of these plants that for two years we held picking parties in June. The berries, caressed with sugar and cream, tasted like mouthfuls of captured sunlight. We ate some that way, but I preferred making jam of them, using "Katisha's Heavenly Strawberry Jam" recipe from the first *Gourmet* magazine cookbook:

> Put 4 cups of hulled, whole berries into a kettle with 5 cups of sugar. Let stand for three hours. Bring to boil over very low fire and boil for 8 minutes. Add 1/2 cup of lemon juice and boil just 2 minutes longer. Pack and seal.

This recipe usually jelled, but not always and not at once. It needed to stand for a month or two. Also, there was a great deal more juice than berries, so jars were always one-third berries floating on two thirds of a jar of jelly or juice. I tried cooling the jars upside down; the berries ended up on the bottom. No matter. The jelly or juice was always delicious and tasted like ripe strawberries.

You can't get this flavor, or any other delicate fruit flavor, such as red raspberry, in commercial jam. Not even in the ones advertised as "all natural" or "all fruit." I looked at the ingredients of several such jams to see why this would be. Most jars of strawberry jam acknowledged the presence of three or more of these ingredients in addition to strawberries and sugar: corn syrup, cranberry juice, unsweetened grape or apple juice concentrates and plums. The finished product tastes like a purée of prunes combined with essence of tobacco. The packers of jams add those extraneous natural ingredients to improve the looks of the product at the expense of taste. They have to do this. Their customers prefer what looks good. We prefer what tastes good.

The poor flavor of American jams wouldn't be so discouraging if the British didn't make commercial jams and jellies with the precise flavors of the most delicate fruits. Even the little plastic packs in many restaurants have these fine flavors.

My desire for good preserves with proper flavors justified regular seasons of berry and fruit picking. As strawberries ended, black raspberries began and our wild cherry trees fruited. The wild cherries were *Prunus serotina*, the black cherry, which comes on trees as tall as eighty feet. The wood from black cherry trees is used for cabinetmaking and interior woodwork. The fruits were small, had a fine flavor for eating, when we could find enough low limbs to get a mess of them, but were really nothing if you cooked them. We tried them for jam; they tasted like sugar and pulp.

Mulberries fruited at the same time as wild cherry. We had three kinds of mulberries: red, white and black. Ripe, these berries tasted like melon. They, too, produced tasteless jam. Their virtue was that the birds liked them about as well as they did our cultivated cherries and robbed us of fewer cherries.

The most plentiful and rewarding of our summer berries were black raspberries, *Rubus occidentalis*. Nearly every summer I picked at least a gallon of these superb fruits and made jam. Every hedgerow and wood's edge on our farm had good stands of the canes.

Going to gather these berries was a trip into another world. I wore long, tough jeans so that I could press into the briers without being ripped apart. Picking was a quiet activity. Birds and animals soon grew accustomed to my being there and went about their business. The daddy longlegs thronged among the canes and trolled about, waving their walking-stick feelers. The air was warm and humid and sweet with perfumes of flowers and mowed grass.

Few things are so visible as unripe black raspberries. They are brilliant red. When they ripen, they tend to disappear, to become, in effect, horticultural black holes that are invisible in the hedgerow shadows. The berries grow in clusters of five or six, the central berry tending to ripen first. When all of a cluster are ripe, one pick brings away five or six berries. That is very satisfying.

When the berries are full ripe, they tend to crush or to drop off at a touch. A Great Dane we owned discovered this. She developed a yen for black raspberries and stood at bushes, bouncing berries with her tongue and eating the ones that rolled off.

The trouble with black raspberry jam is its large seeds and the abundance of them. With young teeth, you can chew them and get the nutty flavor. To older teeth, the seeds are a nuisance. And yet the nutty flavor is essential to the jam. How to get the flavor without the nuisance posed the kind of problem a country dweller rejoices in tackling.

The obvious solution, removing the seeds with a food mill, produced a muddy raspberry purée without the nutty flavor. I tried putting the berries in a blender before cooking them. This was some improvement. The blender shredded about a third of the seeds, but that still left an objectionable number whole. Thinking it over, I ran the berries in the blender, put them on with the proper ratio of sugar—six cups of sugar to four of berries—and cooked until the mixture began to thicken. I then sieved out the seeds and finished the jam. It was fine. The cooking and sugar had drawn out the nutty flavor.

❧

Wineberries, *Rubus phoenicolasius*, bear after black raspberries. They may be the most beautiful berry that the fields offer. Full ripe, each berry has the shape of a raspberry and looks like a ruby. Red-brown hairs cover the canes and make them visible from afar.

The wineberry is an escaped berry that originated in China and Japan and seems to prevail here only in zone 6. It is such a favorite with birds that to get berries in any quantities, one must concentrate on picking. A neighbor, rather than we, tried the berries for wine and bottled up a light-bodied red. We tried them for jam and jelly. The result was about as tasteless as mulberry jam.

❧

Our blackberries made up for all of this lack of flavor, but they did it so strongly that they put me off. When I was young, I loved the blackberries we picked in Georgia. The southern blackberry tasted more like the English bramble. Our Pennsylvania berries have a bitter aftertaste.

The canes of our blackberries are almost as murderous as the multiflora rose, and their seeds are the size of birdshot. The best identity I could find for ours was *Rubus laciniatus*. For any who like their flavor, though, these berries are plentiful. Masses of them bloom along the cuts of highways and promise endless buckets of fruit.

Blackberries are easy to locate. When they begin to ripen fruit, their canes turn red and the thickets look gory. Blackberries also give the black hole effect, but against these sanguine canes, the berries show starkly. I suspected that blackberries would make a decent wine, and we had enough of them to use for that.

After blackberries, wild crabapples ripened, then wild grapes. The wild grapes looked and tasted somewhat like Concords, except foxier. Foxy is a queer sort of dusty acid flavor that lingers in jam or jelly and even in wine. We made all of these things with grapes once or twice. If you had no other fruit to use, the grape confections were not impossible, but they weren't very attractive.

∞

My most rewarding adventure with volunteer goodies was with an asparagus. A small plant sprang up beside a concrete fence post on our lane. I recognized it for what it was and wouldn't let anyone cut it. When its stalks, fully leafed and looking like maidenhair fern, tended to fall or be knocked over, I tied them loosely to the fence post.

Each year the clump grew larger. Presently I could gather six or eight stalks of asparagus about the caliber of an index finger. By the time the clump was thirty years old, I was gathering two to three pounds of stalks each summer.

We could not live luxuriously on the riches of our fields, but, it was comforting to reflect that if we gathered and preserved them, we would never starve.

IMPORTED PESTS

∾

Honeysuckle and Kudzu

The instincts that have prompted us to ban the importing of Japanese beetles, Asian fruit flies, Belgian hares, killer bees and other zoological pests either have not operated on plant pests or have come too late to be effective. That may be because it takes so much longer to learn that a plant is a pest.

Consequently, we have pernicious plants that, despite their attractive characteristics—the attributes that led to their being imported in the first place—have so many adverse and actually dangerous qualities that our woods and fields would be better if they had never arrived.

The oldest pest, I suspect, in date of import is *Lonicera japonica*, Japanese honeysuckle. Everyone who doesn't know much about this vine dotes on it. It blooms off and on in most places all summer and fills the air with a wondrous fragrance.

As Gray puts it in his botany, the plant is "encouraged by those who do not value the rapidly destroyed indigenous vegetation." A tolerant man, Gray cannot restrain his impatience about this honeysuckle. He concludes his note: "Unfortunately naturalized from Asia."

I have a notion that many of our Asian plants were sent or brought home by Ernest "Chinese" Wilson on a willy-nilly basis as a part of the tradition that saw Thomas Jefferson shipping plants all over the world and the Lewis and Clark expedition finds being hauled back to Bernard McMahon in Philadelphia. Wilson spend his life sending home plants from China. But something more unusual must have stimulated the spread of honeysuckle throughout the southern states and below a line from west Texas along the bottom of the Great Lakes and across the northern border of Connecticut. Such a plant can certainly spread widely during a century, but will it spread as much without concentrated help?

The area of this dispersion was also the area where most railroads had cut through hilly country, and I surmise that honeysuckle vines were planted to hold the soil on the banks of railroad cuts. There is no reason to think that honeysuckle wouldn't thrive in the Plains states, but with no banks to retain, there was no incentive to plant it there.

Our farm teems with this vine, and we've spent hours rooting it out. It will girdle small trees and kill them, so we must regularly snip it from saplings. Once trunk diameters exceed two inches, the shade of the tree and of its neighbors discourages honeysuckle. Removing honeysuckle requires getting in with your hands and rummaging up roots from as deep as six inches. Honeysuckle travels from root clump to root clump. It reproduces itself in so many different ways—by seed, root spread, layering, cuttings—that containing it is nearly impossible. Given the chance, it will throttle and pull down forests. At a lower level, it will strangle wild raspberries, blackberries, elderberries, wineberries and attractive shrubs.

Fortunately, honeysuckle cannot survive mowing. Where we could mow it regularly, we drove it back and grass replaced it. This still left a lot of vine in rocky places and on the edges of streams where mowers couldn't go. The greatest blessing for controlling honeysuckle has been the string trimmer, which mows everywhere. Regular trimming on great stretches of our brook has eliminated the honeysuckle and encouraged grass and such perennials as sweet rocket.

Kudzu, another import from Asia, need never have been the nuisance it has become. Fortunately for us, this plant is only marginally hardy in our area, and people have—I hope—sense enough not to encourage it here. Having grown up in the South when the kudzu story began, however, I know how even the best intentions in the world can produce the worst disasters.

I first saw kudzu early in the 1930s, when I visited a castlelike mansion contained within walls. The heavily shaded flat areas were covered with a plant the tenant called kudsel vine. I thought it ugly. It was abundant, fast-growing and succulent and had an aroma of grapes. It grew so rapaciously that even in the shady confines of this castle, bales of kudsel vines had to be rooted up regularly.

Those days most of the farmland in Georgia had been destroyed by uninterrupted crops of cotton. The land had not been farmed. It had been mined. It seemed that nothing could ever restore this land to fecundity. Miles of barren wasteland, bleak, dusty and hopeless, stretched through the vast Piedmont and coastal plains of Georgia.

A Mr. Channing Cope, an earnest and good-hearted man who wrote a farm column in an Atlanta paper, through his own investigation and reasoning and reading on the subject, concluded that a plant called kudzu, imported from Japan, which had got it from east Asia early in the nineteenth century, might be the answer. This plant was the kudsel vine, or *Pueraria lobata*.

For several years, with the zeal of a born-again fundamentalist, Mr. Cope hammered home the virtues of kudzu. Others helped him. Kudzu was a quick-growing, ornamental climber, Cope preached, that would also grow in fields like a crop. It produced masses of leaves, vines and seeds, all succulent and nutritious. It would prosper on the worst possible soil, under the worst possible conditions and provide a forage crop that would fatten any livestock nearly as fast as corn. It would hold banks and prevent erosion. Crops not needed for forage, if disked back into fields, would supply a green manure of exceptional richness. Mr. Cope, paeans of ecstatic tribute pouring from him, envisioned the lands of Georgia, from the hills of Habersham to the valleys of Hall, returned to an agricultural Eden.

Kudzu's farinaceous, tuberous roots would restore the earth farmed out by cotton crops. Rich with a grapelike fragrance, ornamentally attractive and quick growing, abundant with succulent, nutritious leaves, kudzu would enrich the earth, yield tons of wholesome forage and bring blessings to one and all.

And the odd thing was that Mr. Cope was absolutely correct. He told not one lie about this plant. It would do everything he said, and more. And he was earnest in his advocacy. I knew him briefly. He was a sweet man who wanted to leave upon the earth a mark of his kindness. And, as has been the case with all of our plant pests, it was the great benefit they brought that was the problem.

From Toccoa to Valdosta, like children following a Pied Piper, Georgia farmers planted kudzu. Initially it lived up to its promise. There were stories of healthy, highly productive dairy herds, of huge returns on the raising of swine, poultry and beef cattle. Fields once a drear gray-brown were now richly green. Where the green manure had been plowed under for several years, land now supported good crops of soybeans, grains and corn. How sweet it was!

But then. It turned out that no habitat was so suited to rattlesnakes as a dense field of kudzu. These snakes objected to being trampled by livestock or disturbed by poultry. The kudzu concealed the serpent until the moment it was stepped on. Snakebite casualties among farm animals rose.

Although kudzu was plowed into fields as green manure, the plows missed the vines in the hedgerows. These vines took off on careers of their own. They grew across highways, making succulent mats that tires, bearing the weight of vehicles, converted into a slippery purée. Cars and trucks hit these stretches and skidded out of control. The vines climbed trees and pulled them down, encased and ripped apart buildings and eliminated walks and lanes. The blight traveled with epidemic speed over four or five southern states.

The South has had to mount a concerted campaign to control and eliminate kudzu. Helped by several years of drought, southern farmers seem to have gotten a grip on the pest, but it has been an ordeal.

Multiflora: The Full Cycle

Several decades ago, in 1948, the Department of Agriculture urged farmers everywhere to plant multiflora roses. *Rosa multiflora*, hardy everywhere in the United States except in the Rocky Mountains and the southwestern deserts, was another plant that, according to Gray, was introduced from East Asia where, presumably, some natural enemy kept it in check.

The multiflora is, in many ways, a beautiful shrub. It has a dense rose foliage amid which the new shoots are russet to wine color. Each June, the multiflora blooms in dazzling drifts of four-petaled roses so dense they are like a snowfall. The fragrance is a combination of rose and orange blossom and is as heavy and delicious as the scent of gardenia. In autumn, the plant fruits in haws much like those on the firethorn, though not so densely clustered nor so brightly colored. Birds, especially mockingbirds, love these haws and the briery stalks of the multiflora. By supplying abundant winter food and safe spring nesting places, the bushes attract flocks of birds of many varieties.

When the Department of Agriculture in 1948 urged farmers everywhere to plant this rose, it urged upon us all of these and other virtues. Plant the multiflora! was the cry. The rose will grow to a height of ten feet and to a diameter of twelve. It will make a dense enclosure of living barbed wire so tightly meshed and so murderous that not even a shoat can squeeze through without being torn to shreds. Once you have this hedge, you can stop building fences.

The Farm Bureau encouraged us with bundles of a thousand seedlings at very low prices. The seedlings looked terribly fragile. The above-ground portion was about the size and length of a lollipop stick. The root was a foot long. Our neighbor, Mrs. Fraley, with whom we joined in planting, feared so fragile a seedling would never survive the coarse method we used: crack the earth with a spade, insert the root and close by tramping on it. Playing it safe for the hedge along her lane, she planted each seedling with a dibble and a tablespoonful of Transplantone. Her seedlings shot up like ragweed. Those planted our way took hold more slowly, but few died.

Our neighbor across the road, a canny Scots farmer, refused to follow us into multiflora. He did not know where the drawback might be, but he was certain there would be one. The God of John Knox never made anything so easy as planting a fence instead of building one.

Highway departments were not so wary. The highway trade magazines ran articles showing what a safety factor a median strip could become if planted to multiflora. Out-of-control cars could crash into this prickly hedge, and it would stop them with no more damage than some scratched paint that a wax job could fix. Even the crash would be a parachute landing, for the hedge would yield and reduce the force of impact. Many New England states took the bait and planted their highway median strips.

℅

Once our multiflora bushes achieved size and authority, they did prove as attractive as represented, but they were by no means a fully effective animal barrier. Horses and cattle they might stop, for their murderous briers were concentrated in their upper branches. Briers from ground level up to one foot, however, tended to break away and not to regrow on old shoots, so the hedge would not contain fowls, shoats and other small animals, nor would it keep dogs out. The growth of the hedges tended to be irregular and snaggled. Sheep could crowd through the gaps by leaving some wool behind.

The multiflora hedge, in short, failed as a fence.

Once planted, however, its adverse qualities proliferated unabated. Every haw that a bird ate and evacuated, encapsulated in rich manure, germinated and produced, in two years, another huge and robust shrub. The living barbed wire that multiflora provided in hedgerows it also provided in the middle of fields. Nor was seeding by birds the only process of reproduction. Wherever a branch of multiflora touched the ground, it rooted. From these roots further bushes sprang. In a front field that we left uncultivated, ungrazed and unmowed for two years, the multiflora grew so dense that hunters, clad in leather and heavy canvas, could not cross it without being stripped nearly naked by the briers.

Nor did our prudent Scots neighbor come off unscathed. He avoided the ordeal of planting, but birds sitting on his fences did his planting for him. Soon he had hedges as dense as any of ours.

∾

Long before the Department of Agriculture awoke to the blight it had wished upon the land, we realized that this briery pest had to be controlled. We could control it in fields with regular mowing, but if we allowed the plants to reach any size and density, such control was difficult to establish. The plant thrust up a crown of thick, woody shoots. A rotary or a Mott mower had to run over these crowns several times to shred them back to ground level.

Roses in hedgerows became so inextricably entwined with trees—they climbed into trees as high as twenty to thirty feet—that only laborious removal by hand was effective. That or hogging out the hedgerow, trees and all. In addition to being pernicious in itself, multiflora provided a perfect forcing environment for honeysuckle, wild grape and poison ivy. All of these plants seemed to be profoundly symbiotic, the rose supporting and lifting the grape, ivy and honeysuckle, the ivy and honeysuckle binding the rose to the grape to make it more difficult to remove.

We now have a twenty-five-acre pasture-become-swamp that is impenetrably dense with multiflora, grape and honeysuckle. That it is a fine wildlife refuge is indisputable—but only for certain kinds of wildlife. The fairly brisk brook that flows through it, once the habitat of duck, egret and blue heron, has lost these inhabitants. The rose has grown too dense to allow such large birds to enter and leave safely. The rose also harbors natural predators: raccoons, foxes, groundhogs and snapping turtles.

During the spring, when the earth is wet, one can don gloves and pull out fairly large multiflora, roots and all. A small tractor and a rope will uproot even the very largest bushes. Spring attention of this kind can keep hedgerows fairly clear. Multiflora will grow in a wood, but not well. The bushes in a wood are seldom too large to pull by hand, if tackled in the spring.

Using all of these methods, we have confined multiflora to the edges of our woods and to the swamp: that still leaves us with a considerable nuisance and a constant source of seeds for birds to sow everywhere.

Tardily the Department of Agriculture, hagridden with guilt (one likes to think), recognized the curse that multiflora had become and came forward with an herbicide called Tordon 10K, which everyone hoped would prove specific to multiflora. The confidence that the department had in this product was reflected by the careful instructions given in the Tordon 10K bulletin for the alternative method of eradication: hogging everything out with a bulldozer. It didn't make Tordon 10K sound very promising.

Herbicides are tricky remedies. An herbicide purportedly specific to the multiflora is likely to prove specific to all roses. If eradicating the multiflora meant also eradicating the harmless wild roses, the remedy would be tragic. If it went even further and eradicated trees and other shrubs, owing to not being more than partially specific, using it might produce a catastrophe.

Such a result is not unthinkable. Once Mimi and I tried an herbicide supposed to be specific to honeysuckle. Being skeptical about such products, we applied the herbicide cautiously. We anointed a few leaves of five honeysuckle plants. The honeysuckle died all right. So did four poplar trees and two sassafras whose roots were twined with the honeysuckle.

Since its initial introduction, I've heard no further news of Tordon 10K. As our area is widely infested with the rose, I suspect someone would have used it, if it worked. My feeling is that we are probably stuck with the multiflora. The best we can do is keep the plant in check.

One year, when we had had severe drought, white-tailed deer grown desperately hungry ate a lot of our multiflora down to the roots. We dared to hope. But no. Once the drought was over, deer ignored the multiflora. We must still await a cure.

Meanwhile, we can enjoy the large population of mockingbirds that stay all winter now that multiflora is here.

Nothing endures forever and in time—our time or our children's time—some animal, weather condition or blight may attack multiflora, as such infections have attacked chestnuts, oaks, elms, dogwoods and Scotch pines. Regardless, I hope we have sense enough to prohibit any new planting programs.

The Beautiful Nuisance

Each autumn glowing tapestries of yellow and scarlet, which from a distance look like hammered gold encrusted with rubies, climb high into trees. And people in ecstasy, gazing upon these vines, clasp their hands and call them bittersweet.

And they are wrong.

What they behold is a woody North American climber called *Celastrus scandens*, or a Japanese one, introduced fairly recently, circa 1879, *Celastrus orbiculatus*. Both are members of the Celastraceae or staff-tree family. *C. scandens*, false bittersweet in most literature, is also called waxwork, climbing bittersweet and *bourreau des arbres*, which translates roughly as hangman or executioner of trees.

That is precisely what it is, for all of its autumn splendor. But its story—and its confusion with true bittersweet—is curious.

I believe our native vine, *Celastrus scandens*, which prospers from Quebec to North Carolina and west to South Dakota and New Mexico, is not so overwhelming and robust a plant as *C. orbiculatus*. I reached this surmise because, when I first came to Philadelphia in 1942, the plant oper-ating under the name of bittersweet was in short supply. We could find only one so-called bittersweet vine in our early days on the farm. It climbed a tulip poplar in a back field. Only infrequently and erratically could we cut enough of the berries to bring in for arrangements.

Other things conspired to convince me that *Celastrus scandens* was a rare plant. *The Practical Guide to Successful Farming*, published in 1943, encouraged the view with these words:

> If a market is opening for this type of crop, there is every likelihood that planting along hedgerows, stone walls and other waste areas with bittersweet may allow the individual to add bittersweet berries to the winterberry crop. It is against the law to gather bittersweet berries in New Jersey for sale in order to protect some of our game birds.

This suggests that in 1943, the berry that pheasants and ruffed grouse were said to relish was in short supply. *The Illustrated Encyclopaedia of American Wildflowers*, published in 1947, listed bittersweet as one of the flowers in the northeastern United States and Canada that needed pro-tection. But this book did not mention *Celastrus scandens*. To its authors, bittersweet was *Solanum dulcamara*.

This aroused my curiosity. What was bittersweet, anyhow?

I found that it really was *Solanum dulcamara*, which had a long and colorful history and was about as unlike *Celastrus scandens* as it could be and still resemble it enough to be confused with it.

❧

Celastrus scandens was unknown to European botanists until it was sent over from the American continent. To Europeans, as to the ancient Greeks and Romans, bittersweet was the sprawling vine *Solanum dulca-mara*, a member of the Solanaceae, or nightshade, family. *S. dulcamara* was also called climbing nightshade, scarlet berry, blue bindweed and felonwood and had a bountiful family of cousins: potatoes, tomatoes, egg-plants, Jerusalem cherries and horse nettles. The vine, which grows from

Newfoundland to southern New England and westward to Michigan and Illinois, but not much farther south, has conspicuous violet flowers with green spots, and scarlet berries. Although these berries are colored like *Celastrus scandens* berries, they are ellipsoidal rather than spherical, and much less abundant. In short, the resemblance between the two plants is largely superficial.

Like most plants long known to man, *Solanum dulcamara* has been sampled as both food and medicine with a typically wide disagreement over its virtues. This sampling gave the plant its name, however. Those who tasted it said it was first bitter, then sweet. Hieronymus Bock, a German physicist and botanist (1498–1554), first named the plant *amara dulcis, dulcis amara*, dulcamara. William Turner, in his herbal of 1568, translated this Latin name as bittersweet.

❧

Solanum dulcamara did not grow in North America when our colonists arrived. It was brought from Europe later. What our colonists saw and gathered for decorative arrangements was *Celastrus scandens*. Because it somewhat resembled *S. dulcamara*, they called it bittersweet. Had any who had tasted the berries of *S. dulcamara* and found them bittersweet tasted the berries of *C. scandens*, as I have, they could have avoided the error. I can't find that *C. scandens* berries have much taste at all beyond a somewhat grassy, herbage type of flavor. Certainly there is nothing like Gerard's description, in his herbal, of the flavor of *S. dulcamara*: "...of a sweet taste at first but after, of a strong savour..."

Even so, that we confused the two plants and have now come to regard *Celastrus scandens* as bittersweet is of no great consequence, especially when true bittersweet is rather scarce. The concept of bittersweet is so appealing that we have named plays and books, songs, foods and chocolates bittersweet and, whenever we have illustrated these items, the picture has been of *C. scandens*.

Or of *Celastrus orbiculata*.

It is this second member of the family that threatens trouble. By the time various writers were remarking the shortage of bittersweet and rec-

ommending its planting, C. *orbiculata* had been in the country for about
sixty-five years. I can't find that anyone had compared the relative hardiness and growth rate of the two vines, but circumstantial evidence suggests
that C. *orbiculata* must be twice or three times as hardy and prolific as C.
scandens.

Where we once had very little *Celastrus scandens*, we now have bales
of bittersweet, most of it C. *orbiculata*. This Asian species has berry clusters on the leaf axils of the current year's growth, but they are substantially
hidden until the leaves fall; the native C. *scandens* has berry clusters in terminal panicles or racemes and these are continually visible.

Most weed pests are immediately identifiable in all seasons. Multiflora
has thorns; honeysuckle wraps around everything tightly and densely;
kudzu has succulent leaves and a strong fragrance of grape; poison ivy has
its three green leaves and stems that bind themselves to a host with a
dense mesh of rootlets. Bittersweet, by which from here on we will mean
the Celastraceae, is secretive until it gets its brilliant autumn colors. It
issues no odor or perfume, has no thorn or poison and, initially, does not
bind its host closely.

To follow the course of bittersweet, one must identify a robust plant in
autumn, mark its location and come back in spring. Because the plants are
dioecious—having flowers of only one sex on individual specimens—the
male plant is always difficult to identify. Although a male vine can bear a
few female flowers, these seldom produce enough berries to draw attention. Once one grows accustomed to the look of them, however, the vines,
leaves and berries are recognizable in all seasons.

When small, the vines have a grayish brown bark with ridges running along it. On stems thicker than a quarter inch in diameter, the ridges
are gone, and the bark has turned light brown and is pocked with irregularly spaced pores. The sawtooth edges of the succulent green leaves dis-
tinguish them from honeysuckle leaves, which are smaller and have
smooth edges. Bittersweet tends to run straight for greater distances and to
wind loosely around limbs and branches.

Dense woods tend to shade and kill honeysuckle, but bittersweet,
which grows up with the trees, lives on. Perhaps this technique of growing

with the host is a reason for the early looseness of the vine nooses. The thickening growth of the host tightens the choke collar and produces the throttling effect.

With its roots firmly fixed in the earth, the bittersweet keeps its green leaves, blossoms and fruits on the tops of trees in a wood. The bark of very old vines peels like dried paint. Vines in the wood are easy to cut, and they should be cut. High above, they will be throttling a tree. Though their berries may feed a bird or two, they are too high for pheasants or grouse and no human eye will ever enjoy them.

Hear the Bush-Browns in *America's Garden Book* on the subject of uncontrolled bittersweet:

> ...although loved for the brilliant coloring and decorative
> qualities of its fruit...[the Celastraceae have] a propensity
> to clamber over surrounding trees and shrubs and, in time,
> will cause considerable damage. Pruning will keep it in
> control; cutting it down or spraying it with brush killer will
> eliminate it.

And yet these are probably our loveliest and most effective materials for autumn and dried-flower arrangements. They hold their brilliant yellow and red-orange fruits all winter and longer.

The vines are easy to cut, to shape and to manage. No need to go after them with brush killer. Clipping all plants except the ones we wish to use should keep bittersweet in control.

BUILDING AND PLANTING THE LIBRARY WING

❧

Building

After fifteen years of prudent expenditure and investments of sweat equity, we had paid off the money we had borrowed to buy our farm, and I had achieved a good income. Each year we had some discretionary capital to put aside. We reached the time to expand. If we were to have the visual pleasure of a farm like Hebe Dick's, we would have to make our own that attractive.

That was the aesthetic reason. There were practical reasons. The one thing that a writer does not stint himself on is the purchase of books. He may suffer tattered underwear or too few pajamas, but he will buy books. In our youth, both Mimi and I had the habit of skimping on movies and other delights to buy books we wanted. Now that we were married, we might think twice about buying a lamp or a chair, a pot or a pan, even a can of paint, but never about a book. Our zeal for buying books had increased our library to well over two thousand volumes. They were stacked all over the house. We had nowhere to put them. And we now had three sons, one bathroom and no laundry.

Before we tackled enlarging the house, however, we did the ha-ha wall, imitating Mrs. Dick's arrangement of separating the house and its terrace from the pasture. We built a part of the wall, had earth from the lane and a new turnaround pushed behind it, then finished the wall.

That sounds easy. It wasn't. We lived for eighteen months in a sea of mud, a no-man's-land of hardpan studded with granite boulders and shattered tree roots. Much of the time our only access to our house was over planks that bridged small chasms. We spent our spare time gathering stones and stacking them in cairns. We were going to be building a lot of wall.

When the time came to build the first sections of wall, we bought a concrete mixer driven by a one-horsepower gasoline engine and hired an Italian mason, Angelo Sparano. He was from Naples, he said. He was the only dour Neapolitan I had ever met. Smiling was hard for him. He also had trouble accepting the idea of Mimi's running the mixer and supplying him with mortar, but Mimi, a frustrated mason, was insistent. The first and longest sections of wall took six months and changed the entire look of our farm. The visual lines of the wall pulled everything together. In a small way, we were duplicating the Hanging Gardens of Babylon.

We were careful to design our terrace so we could drive our Jeep truck and power equipment anywhere on it. The major work on a farm is hauling things from one place to another. Doing it with a wheelbarrow is pointless labor, if you can do it with a tractor and a cart. Besides, many loads are too large or too unwieldy to move except in a truck or a trailer.

∽

With the worst of the wall done, we were ready to plan our wing. We could not afford the architects who made a profession of restoration. Their charges were very high and they insisted on the prohibitively expensive procedures and techniques intended to reproduce precisely Colonial construction. The degree of exactness always seemed prissy nonsense to me. If George Washington could have painted Mount Vernon in titanium white instead of white lead, I am sure he would have. He would also have rejoiced in electric light and central heating.

We engaged an architect with more general experience. From him we learned a lot about the ways creative design can conflict with what is practical and with what will work when you have to live with it day in and day out.

Mimi told our architect we wanted what she called an educated barn: a wing that would be solid walls except for the center third, which would be all windows, front and back. We soon found that the contemporary architect of the 1950s understood the designs of school buildings, development houses and split-level ranches. He was also a wizard with weird architectural geometry. But about designing a workable country house for the mid-Atlantic United States he hadn't a clue. That generality may be a little severe, but I don't think our architect was a freak. I think probably he was average.

He brought us, first, a wing substantially made of glass that had a reflecting basin, half of which was in the living room and half of which was outdoors. We told him that this would be the finest arrangement imaginable for bleeding heat out of a house on winter days. We also asked him where our books were going to go with all of these glass walls. Books? Oh!

The only windows in his next design were a row of transoms up in the eaves. All else was given over to bookcases. A massive wall would stand between us and the beautiful view of our pasture.

In his next design, he got the windows in the middle of the wing, but he devised a roof that was complicated beyond belief. Its main gable ran east and west. Over the central section, where the windows would be, three parallel gables, each a window's width, ran north and south. From the top it would look like a cross with three crosspieces, similar to the cross of Lorraine. The architect's details for the structure of this roof showed joints where as many as sixteen beams would meet. The contractor killed this. There wasn't a roof man in the state who would put up that roof and guarantee it.

Our staircase was going to move from our old house to our wing. By now we had a model of the wing. We kept moving the staircase around, seeking the best traffic pattern with the least wasted space. The architect's final, triumphant scheme gave us a conservatory on top of the downstairs powder room, a space ten by ten feet. We filled the area with gravel. It turned out to be the only place in the wing where the sun never shone. The cats used it for a litter box.

Another novelty the architect introduced into his drawings was the permanent woodpile. He made much of a large pile of firewood that he had drawn on a terrace. A beautiful design feature! When I pointed out that by spring each year we would have used it up, he was dumbfounded.

Frequently, he enunciated his devout hope that we would not "drape" the windows. "Drapes" would destroy the look of the design. Of course we did hang draperies because they provided an effective heat barrier, as every good housekeeper knows. Conserving heat was much more important than bowing to architectural prejudices.

I suspect all building is like this, though, and we were fortunate to get, for the most part, our educated barn with bookcases around most of its second floor. Because the second floor was a balcony, the space was dramatic, which was what we wanted.

A surprising number of people looked at it and, after the theatrical effects wore off, exclaimed: "Just think what you could have had, if you'd made it into bedrooms!"

"I have thought," I answered. "A hotel."

∾

We lived in the house while it was being enlarged and modified. We couldn't afford to do the house and live elsewhere. It was like living on a stage in a theater where they kept changing the set for some such large production as *Les Misèrables*. The only room that didn't get changed was the kitchen.

When they took out the old staircase, there was a week when any of us could have fallen forty feet, from the attic to cellar. We were constantly shifting bedrooms as the workmen moved from one to another. They took out the old bathroom before they finished the new bathroom. For ten days we had no place to bathe. We moved our old bathtub to the new cellar under the wing, hooked it to the water taps installed to feed the washing machine, and emptied the tub into the floor drain. It was kind of like bathing on a station platform where wild winds blew and trains were expected hourly.

When the wing was done, we had all these delicious new bathrooms and closets, all this lovely new space. Our electrical system had once run through eight fuse boxes in the cellar. When a fuse blew, finding it was an adventure. Now we had two banks of circuit breakers. We had never been able to have a laundry in the original house. There wasn't space for it. Now we had an ample one in the cellar. Our bookshelves offered us space for four thousand books, so our library disappeared into them.

What we didn't have was enough furniture. Our rooms looked like those classic stagings for Shakespeare where the whole set is two chairs, twenty feet apart, in front of a curtain.

The vast space inside was dwarfed by vaster space outside. For a while we were occupied with filling in earth behind our ha-ha walls. When that was done, we faced a major planting job, the job that we hoped would be an inheritance for our boys. As we worked on it, horticulture began to influence the growth of our library.

My own library had been devoted to contemporary and classic fiction, biographies of authors and bound volumes of magazines, among them *National Geographic*, which offered a good deal of horticulture. Mimi's library had been Irish lore and legends, King Arthur and many volumes of memoirs of the courts of Europe.

When we moved to the country, we began to pick up such books as we could on gardening. I ordered a *Gray's Botany*, and Mimi bought the superb basic gardening book by the Bush-Browns, *America's Garden Book*. We went on from there to *Joy of Gardening*, by Vita Sackville-West, *Garden in Your House* by Ernesta Drinker Ballard, Gerard's *Herbal* and the fine collection of books on trees and wood by Eric Sloane. Once we started, we bought with such zeal that books on horticulture and related subjects were about a fifth of our holding

We bought *Hortus Third* when it appeared, the thirty-volume Roger

Tory Peterson guides, six or eight books on mushrooms, McPhee's *Oranges*, Rodale's and other herbals and illustrated encyclopedias of trees and shrubs.

Our interest brought us into the Pennsylvania Horticultural Society and encouraged us to go regularly to Longwood Gardens, where we researched the plants we would need for borders and gardens.

Mimi deserves credit for the success of our adventures. She had come to the country with only a superficial knowledge of horticulture, although she had a profound love of flowers. She had never studied either Latin or Greek. Yet she learned rapidly the botanical names for a vast array of flowers and shrubs. She learned these simply by rote, but she did such a thorough job that we seldom encountered a plant she couldn't identify.

Excitement ran high for her when January came and the garden catalogues began to arrive. She beguiled wintry, snowy evenings ordering paper birches; filberts, including the filbert called Sir Harry Lauder's walking stick, *Corylus avellana contorta*; *Fritillaria liliacea*; and other exotica. One year she grew *Luffa*, the vegetable sponge the British know as loofah, and made the front page of the *Wall Street Journal* in a round-up story about unusual horticulture.

Mimi seized on each catalogue, each book as it came and read it. She had a zeal for reading horticultural dictionaries. Mimi read even such volumes as *Gray's Botany* like somebody whipping through a detective novel. This led us to many horticultural adventures, one of the first being English box, because Mimi had read it was elegant and difficult to grow.

A Career of English Box

When our ha-ha wall was finished, we could stand on it anywhere and stare into unobstructed distance like a Navajo scouting from some ancient butte. In an enclosed society, this would never do. Horticulturally, we were naked.

We talked a great deal about what to plant. Whatever we chose, we would need a lot of it. That made the expense sound prohibitive. Then, one evening, I came home and found Mimi full of excitement. She had discovered English box on sale at 50 cents per plant and had bought a hundred plants. I was impressed. These were not shabby plants. Each was six inches high and well leafed; each had a nice root structure. We struck a line five feet back from the wall and planted our box bushes eight inches apart. They looked pathetically small and vulnerable.

The winds of winter visited them harshly, yellowing their leaves. Dogs and children snapped off two or three at ground level. The snaggled result seemed unlikely to produce the lushly verdant hedge we hoped for. The plants seemed, in fact, unlikely to endure at all, for English box was delicate. I knew them of old.

❧

When I had reached my sixth birthday, my Uncle Howell took me on the languid voyage that the sidewheeler *Charles McAllister* made from the Anacostia tidal basin down the Potomac to Mount Vernon. What impressed me most about Mount Vernon was a number of large, dense shrubs, billowing masses of dark green foliage, that looked as if they should be in a Maxfield Parrish mural instead of out in the open. I asked Uncle Howell what they were.

"Box," he said. "Box bushes."

"Are they used to make boxes?"

"Yes." Uncle Howell was a tease. "Cigar boxes."

Supposing that all of it originated at Mount Vernon, I became a great admirer of the wood in cigar boxes. It was years before I realized that there weren't enough box bushes on earth to supply the wood for the number of cigar boxes on earth and that the wood in cigar boxes was cedar.

❧

In Atlanta, where I grew up, there was a house where a Mrs. Goodrum dwelt. On each side of the broad walk leading to her front door stood a hedge of English box, each bush about five feet high and five feet through. Mrs. Goodrum had bought her box full grown, of course, rather as one might buy matched pearls. They were breathtakingly beautiful. They were also an expensive nuisance. Each winter she had to have them caged in wooden frames with hemp bagging stretched over them. Even then some winters yellowed them.

The only box bushes I had ever seen growing to large sizes with little attention in zone 6, our zone, were individual bushes in moderate shade on the north sides of houses or in deep shade on the other sides.

Our hundred box bushes were not planted in any such sheltered place.

They stood in the broad sunlight and in the path of every wind, no matter how cold or how strong. The Latin name for box, *Buxus sempervirens* (evergreen) var. *suffruticosa,* had better be accurate, or we were heading for a row of one hundred brown stubs.

By now, our horticultural library had grown enough to allow some research. I checked out this box. Although the shrub was called English box, it came originally from southern Europe, Asia and Japan. The Romans cultivated it long before anyone but aborigines had set foot in England.

The sobriquet *English* came from the extensive use of box in England in seventeenth- and eighteenth-century cloister garths, castle bowers and town yards with their knot gardens, borders and mazes. The shrub thrived in England's moist climate and mild winters.

We had no such climate. If we were to keep our box, we were going to have to protect it from winter wind and most winter sunlight, particularly morning sunlight. We began organizing protection the year after we planted our hedge. We brought from our wood three wild dogwoods and planted them between the box and the wall. As the dogwoods grew spreads of branches, the health of our hedge improved. The trees acted as a kind of lath house, breaking the force of the winter winds, diffusing the light of the sun. The box suffered less winter burn and lost less of the previous year's growth.

Two years later we did the planting that made the ultimate difference. Against the stone ha-ha wall, we planted a second hedge of Hicks yew, *Taxus baccata* 'Hicksii', leaving between the hedges the three feet of space in which the dogwoods stood. From the moment this second hedge went in, the box stopped suffering winter burn, even in the disastrous 1976–77 and 1981–82 winters, when we logged periods of subzero nights.

As our hedge prospered, I found that revisiting the cloudland of English box was better than my original visit. The foliage was as incredibly rich green as I had remembered, and there was a fragrance that I hadn't remembered because I hadn't been close enough to box before.

There are those who despise the odor of English box. It smells, they say, like cats. I can see what they mean. If you get a really heavy whiff from right among the leaves, it smells as if a tomcat has sprayed. But diluted by a little distance, the fragrance seems to me more like freshly engraved dollar bills.

Box should smell like money. The mature shrubs, pound for pound, are among the more valuable plants in horticulture. The shrub grows slowly: two to three inches per year in the favorable climates of England, Virginia, Maryland and the Carolinas and little more than an inch per year in our climate. Hence, English box of any size, having had to be aged like wine and protected constantly against temperature and other shocks, is, like aged wine, quite costly. Shrubs measuring a foot high by a foot through bring $50 to a $100 each. For larger bushes, there isn't a price. You negotiate.

This is why *Buxus sempervirens* must be a career for any but the very rich and a heritage for heirs.

By the end of its eighth year our own hedge had become a foot tall. The individual bushes had grown together. We had taken out the ones that had broken off at ground level and transferred them to a nursery bed with maximum protection from the weather. They had nearly overtaken the plants in the hedge.

We noticed that once the plants in the hedge grew together, their growing slowed. Because we now had other places for box, we began to transplant every other box, leaving the remaining plants sixteen inches apart and spacing the transplants sixteen inches. This gave us hedges in which the individual bushes had a curiously mashed look: ten to twelve inches tall and through but only six to eight inches wide. Freed from constraints, each bush flourished on its narrow sides and, in a year or two, was round again.

By now we had confirmed without doubt box's name of evergreen. The plants that the children and the dogs had broken off at ground level had grown back as full as the ones that hadn't been broken. Plants that lost major branches regrew them. Five of our original plants, grown in the increasing shade of a Pfitzer's juniper, had died back to three-inch stubs before we rescued them. Two of the five had no leaves. We transferred them to the nursery. In five years each had grown back to ten inches tall and ten inches through.

∾

In addition to being burned by bad weather, our box was also attacked by other problems. On several occasions, yellow jackets built nests near the roots of a box and used the bush itself as a thoroughfare to the nest. This usually produced a tuft of dead leaves at the exit. When winter came and the yellow jackets died, we cut out the tufts and the plant gradually filled itself in.

Over winter months big sections of a large box may turn brown or yellow and die. Horticulturists blame this on a disease engendered by an accumulation of trash (dead leaves, grass) in the major crotch of the bush. The disease girdles branches and kills them. The only remedy is to remove the diseased branches all the way back to the crotch, clean the crotch and treat it with a disinfectant. This was troublesome, but it seemed to work.

Another cause of this dieback may be allowing masses of dead leaves to lie on the box all winter. I have observed that the box tends to turn brown beneath these leaves if I don't remove them.

Cut back, a blighted box looks fairly tacky, but though box does not grow rapidly, it does grow resolutely. Given time, it will fill in.

Being fairly shallow rooted, apart from its sturdy taproot, English box is easily transplanted. Put into a favorable environment, the bush will show no ill effects from the move. We've thinned our original hedge three times, losing only one transplant that we put into an impossible place. By the time we began our third thinning, the plants in our original hedge were four feet apart, more than three feet tall and three feet in diameter.

At this point we had to stop thinning and replanting. We were running out of places for hedges. Consider: we set our first hundred plants eight inches apart and got a hedge nearly seventy feet long. Thinned until all of the plants were sixteen inches apart, our hundred box made a hedge nearly one hundred thirty-five feet long. By the third thinning we had begun to set the transplants four feet apart; a five-box line was twenty feet long, and our original hundred plants were sufficient for a four-hundred-foot hedge.

According to the Bush-Browns, left unclipped and raised in a favorable environment, a box will grow twelve to fifteen feet tall and twenty-five feet through. A hedge of a hundred such bushes would be more than eight times the length of a football field.

This argued in favor of letting our four-foot shrubs grow together and stabilize. From now on, if we want our bushes to hold their size, probably we will prune. We had needed more than thirty years to reach this point. That's why I say that growing English box is a career.

In England and in our mid-Atlantic states, *Buxus sempervirens* puts out new growth twice: in the spring and in the autumn. In Pennsylvania, frost usually nips the second growth, so our box grows only half as fast as bushes in more favored climates. Although *B. sempervirens* will tolerate the most severe kind of clipping, if the object is to allow the shrubs to continue growing, they shouldn't be clipped until the spring growth has matured, and the clipping should be directed toward shaping. If the object is to hold the hedge at the same size, the plants should be allowed the refreshment of their spring growth, then clipped back to their original size. There are box hedges that have been kept ten inches high for seventy-five years. The best time to clip, either to shape or to maintain bush size, seems to be about mid-June.

Few of us can afford to put down the wine cellars that our ancestors did, but all of us can leave our heirs an abundant heritage of English box, which is always a joy to behold, a fragrance of riches and, in time of dire need, money in the bank.

Yew, the Ancient One

We planted a hedge of Hicks yew to protect our investment in English box. To reach us as Hicks yew, this shrub had to travel a long route.

The yew of legend and story is the English yew, *Taxus baccata*, which was native to most of the northern hemisphere except North America. Specimens of this yew fifteen hundred years old still exist, and fossil remains from the Tertiary have been unearthed.

The name *Taxus* is Latin for yew tree or bow. The English name *yew* is from the Welsh *yw*, which is appropriate. Yew flourishes in Wales. One of eight species of dioecious evergreens and shrubs with thin leaves and pinkish scarlet, succulent fruits called axils, *Taxus baccata*, though slow growing, reaches heights of seventy feet. Its wood, dense, strong and pliable, was valued for wood carving and for longbows. They were yew bows with which the English archers won the battle of Agincourt.

Probably *Taxus baccata* was brought here from Europe. Thomas Jefferson, who planted it on the west side of Monticello, first saw it at Hampton

Court, near London, and wrote that he was shipping home "3 doz. Dwarf Ewe to be planted among the Kentucky coffee trees." He called the plant English yew. What he knew as American yew was *T. canadensis*.

Taxus canadensis is a straggling evergreen, rarely as tall as seven feet, found in rich woods from Newfoundland to West Virginia and westward through Kentucky to Iowa. It continues to grow in the wild, but no great horticultural use has been found for it.

∾

Before Christianity came to Britain, the Druids considered *Taxus baccata* a sacred tree and built their temples near yews. The Celts, in addition to getting longbows from yew wood, used the sap to poison their arrows. Yews contain the toxic alkaloid taxine, which makes all parts of it, especially the leaves and seeds, poisonous, so deadly that fifty of the small leaves are said to be a lethal dose.

During the reign of Edward I, yews were planted in English churchyards to defend churches against damage from high winds. These ecclesiastical trees grew quite large. One at Crowhurst, noted by Sir John Evelyn, had reached a thirty-foot circumference by 1910; the one at Ankerwyke exceeded that by another three inches. With time, the hardwood in these yews deteriorates, leaving hollow centers.

Taxus baccata in its original form was favored for planting both as specimens and in hedges and was used extensively for topiary. The ideal yew didn't evolve, however, until we imported *T. cuspidata* from Japan and crossed it with *T. baccata* to produce a variety of cultivars, among which was *T. × media* 'Hicksii', an ideal hedge and topiary shrub that flourishes from zone 5 to zone 8.

Hicks yew has a natural columnar shape and the advantage of rapid growth. Unchecked, it will grow to twenty feet in ten years. The rapid growth plus its hardiness from the Great Lakes to southern Georgia have made Hicks yew an extremely attractive hedging plant.

We planted it on our farm in 1960, putting in eighty young plants six inches tall and four inches through. We now have two hedges that total two hundred fifty feet long and are five feet tall and five feet through.

We put our original plants three feet apart in a soil that was mainly clay. We watered the hedge diligently the first two years, then left it to nature. At first the planting looked straggly, but in five years it had grown so dense that we couldn't see through it. Clipping it once a year has kept it at the five-by-five size.

Because our hedge runs from bright sunlight through light shade to dense shade, it provides a continuing case history on the plants' reaction to sunlight. The parts in bright sun flourish with rude, thrusting vigor, the side facing the sun doing twice as well as the side away from it. When the hedge runs under trees, it grows less densely and more slowly in proportion to the density of the shade. A point in Hicks yew's favor is that it grows steadily in all of these conditions.

Where Hicks yew is used for display topiary, as in the great hedges and sculptured animals at Longwood Gardens, the clipping produces large horizontal surfaces. These surfaces please the eye, but they also collect snow that may break the bush, if you have no staff of gardeners to clear away the snow. We diminish the danger by clipping our yews to rounded tops and sides, striking the line of the top and rounding down from that level. The time to clip is after the major new growth has occurred, in late July or early August. Properly maintained, a yew hedge probably is the prettiest and most effective barrier you can have. Its surface is denser, finer and greener than privet.

❧

Two other yew cultivars are of interest. *Taxus baccata* 'Standishii', which grows to twenty-five feet and tolerates shearing, is hardy in zones 6 and 7 and has branches that begin yellow and produce golden leaves that fade to yellow-green. *T. baccata* 'Repandens', a nearly prostrate shrub with blue-green leaves, makes a fair ground cover and a good edging plant.

Yews may be taken up and transplanted in April. Yew seeds are solitary and contained in the fleshy red axils, which are attractive to bees and yellow jackets. The flesh of these axils is the only nonpoisonous part of the yew.

Like all poisonous plants, yews tempted man to explore their medicinal properties, killing off a good many patients in the process until the discovery of taxol, used in modern cancer treatments. The alkaloid taxine, extracted, desiccated to white crystals and dissolved in alcohol or ether, was once used to depress blood circulation. Indians, knowing only *Taxus canadensis*, used minute quantities of toxic leaf tea both externally and internally for rheumatism, bowel ailments, scurvy and as a diuretic.

These morbid properties probably prompted poets to write such words as Ben Jonson's:

> *What gentle ghost besprent with April dew,*
> *Hails me so solemnly to yonder yew.*

or Robert Blair's in *The Grave*:

> *Careless, unsocial plant that loves to dwell*
> *Midst shells and coffins, epitaphs and worms.*

But Mimi regularly admired what she called the "uneven undulations of unclipt yew." Ancient stands of *T. baccata* are indeed glorious. At Powys Castle in Welshpool, Wales, the country where yew got its common name, yews ascend thirty to fifty feet, clipped to smooth cones. One hedge is fifty yards long and three stories high. The fine-leafed surface of these yews is a stunning, brilliant green and much too gay for death.

Miniclimates

The orientation of our new wing, the pool, and the pool house gave us, serendipitously, a variety of what the horticultural world was beginning to call miniclimates. Because this was a new and made-up word, it could mean whatever we wished it to mean, but young words, like young children, ought to be nourished with some care to avoid spoiling them.

In the broadest sense a miniclimate is a condition that prevails naturally in one small spot and differs from the surrounding climate. It is distinct from such confected miniclimates as those in cold frames and conservatories in that it occurs out-of-doors subject to weather and protected only by its site. This did not mean that a miniclimate could not be established deliberately. The first ones we saw, at Longwood Gardens, were deliberate. On a knoll in the rock garden built in the early 1960s, Longwood made a small alpine garden by heavily irrigating the exposed knoll and planting it to mountain flowers. Later, it turned out, the entire rock garden—a horseshoe of cliffy, rocky ledges—because its open end faced west, contained a miniclimate. Southern magnolias, *Magnolia grandiflora*, grew in the shelter of the cliff, bloomed each year and suffered damage only in severe winters.

Longwood were so pleased with this result that they established in an appropriate area an outdoor bog garden that harbored insect-eating plants: another deliberate miniclimate.

Obviously, such outdoor miniclimates cannot bring the magnificent spectacles that one can get in the controlled atmosphere of greenhouses and conservatories nor even the rewarding abundance of cold frames. Nor will miniclimates provide flowers or fruits out of season. But they will provide the startling and improbable appearance of flowers, shrubs and trees in places where they should not be expected to survive. For the earnest horticulturist, this is great fun.

It is also a satisfaction of an atavistic wish that prevails in the human mind and spirit and produces such fantasies as *Lost Horizon*'s Shangri-La: the hope that spring and summer will come in winter—or that little smatterings of them will. For these reasons, many of us will cultivate, at least briefly, the Christmas rose, a plant so resolutely hardy that it will bloom beneath snow and will smile up in January, if we will go out and brush away the snow. Plants that carry over in a miniclimate in places where winter is supposed to kill them seem, by such small miracles, to reaffirm the belief in the resurrection. Hence the most rewarding and exciting miniclimates are those that occur by accident—those that are discovered, like a small patch of lost treasure.

Our first and most straightforward application of miniclimate began with our English box. Had we left our box exposed, probably all of them would have died. But we created a lath house with trees and established windbreaks and barriers with other shrubs.

One could argue, of course, that this was a borderline example of miniclimate, that it amounted to little more than selecting a suitable exposure, as one must for azaleas and rhododendrons. But on small scales we have managed, often as much by accident as by design, to establish unexpected pockets of miniclimate. In several outdoor places on our farm impatiens reseed themselves and return every year, although our climate is supposed to be too cold for this. In pockets on the front of the old part of our house, we grow three nandina plants, which are unprotected except by their location. I could not say that these plants thrive, although in some years they do rather well. On the other hand, they haven't died, which I take to be one of the criteria of success in a miniclimate.

The Eleagnus Adventure

W hen the building of fine houses flour-
ished in the years following World War II, seeking new plants and shrubs
for decoration and permanent planting became popular. People were
bored with privet, mock orange, pampas grass and even cannas. What
could they have instead?

Some early candidates were barberry and euonymus for hedges and
firethorn for wall decoration. In Atlanta, where I grew up, although
wealthy people could put in and maintain English box, doing so was too
expensive and troublesome. The gardeners there, seeking alternatives,
came up presently with *Elaeagnus pungens,* a member of a family of shrubs
and trees of varying hardiness. All but one of these came from Europe or
Asia.

Although the Elaeagnaceae were not a big family, the naming of them
seemed as confused as if they had been a big family. The five main species
were *angustifolia, commutata* (or *argentea*), *umbellata, multiflora* (or *longipes*)
and *pungens.*

Elaeagnus pungens, the variety that appealed to Atlanta gardeners, was evergreen in Atlanta, bore a heavy bloom of white blossoms in October and, by the following May, matured ellipsoidal, pinkish red berries splotched with silver. Pretty dramatic. Obviously, if you could grow a plant as sensational as this, you would do it. Its leaves were lance shaped and had many points on their edges, as holly does. The leaves even curled irregularly in somewhat the fashion of English holly.

Atlantans planted *Elaeagnus pungens* on banks everywhere. It grew with rampaging vigor to bushes twelve feet high and about the same in diameter. I have seen these huge plantations of *E. pungens* in blossom and in fruit. They are a sight either way. We think that a mass blooming of honeysuckle is impressive in the way it fills the air with fragrance. Well, *E. pungens* can top it.

Elaeagnus pungens was the only eleagnus that had been crossed to any useful purpose. The Dutch had developed five crosses: 'Aurea' (rich yellow leaf margin), 'Fruitlandii' (large rounded leaves with wavy margins), 'Maculata' (large yellow blotch in the center of the leaf), 'Simonii' (leaf variegated with yellow and pinkish white) and 'Variegata' (leaf margins of yellow and white).

My mother, who lived in Atlanta, admired *Elaeagnus pungens* and planted it around her house.

The quantity of ellipsoidal berries on *Elaeagnus pungens* must have been huge in Atlanta and the germination rate must have been equally high, for presently Mother was incessantly having to thin her *E. pungens*. She didn't like to throw away seedlings, so she sent them to us. Four or five times per year, either packaged separately or crammed into boxes bearing Christmas or birthday presents, Mother forwarded seedlings of *E. pungens*. She packed so badly that most of the seedlings arrived dead, but like the great migrations of floating coconuts among the tropical islands, with so many individuals traveling there had to be survivors.

Mimi potted the surviving plants, raised them to ten-inch bushes and popped them into various sheltered locations around our house where a miniclimate might exist. *Elaeagnus pungens* proved marginally hardy. Four plants in four environments survived and grew eight to ten feet tall.

They bloomed abundantly, bore fruit and produced a few seedlings. These surviving shrubs had either a northeast or southwest exposure and were completely sheltered from winter wind and winter sun. Each was against a wall or a lattice barrier.

Because the growth was slow and damage was almost certain to any branch that *Elaeagnus pungens* thrust beyond its safe environment, we avoided the drawbacks that Atlantans had with this plant. There, the shrubs had to be clipped regularly and severely. *E. pungens* being wickedly thorned, this clipping was not a comfortable job. Also, Atlantans had to control the prolific reseeding.

Although our plants were evergreen, one, somewhat more exposed to winter winds than the others, became deciduous and still survived for three years. It blossomed and bore fruit until it died.

The glories of the *E. pungens* that lived were impressive. New leaves appeared in spring just as the fruit was maturing. These new leaves, a dark, olive green on top and silver on the bottom, made a startling contrast to the pink-red silver-flecked fruit. By autumn, the leaves were a lighter green marked with silver gray and were so distinctive that, wherever you encountered one, you recognized it. Each was an elongated lance shape with sides that tended to curl under. By autumn, the undersides had taken on a powdering of rusty gold.

Among these leaves, thousands of small white blossoms, each no more than three eighths of an inch long, hung like limp opera gloves and filled the air with an exotic fragrance that seemed to me like a powerful carnation talcum. Other horticulturists found the fragrance like gardenias; still others, like lilies. When other flowers were dead and the prevailing aroma was of acorns, fermenting leaves and grasses, the perfume of *Elaeagnus pungens* echoed spring.

Though our experience with *Elaeagnus pungens* was refreshing, in giving us a novelty for several years, and tended to try the effectiveness of some of our miniclimates, we found that in the long run even a miniclimate couldn't protect it in severe winters. Mother is long gone and so are the eleagnus she sent us.

Hollies

One needs no miniclimate in the Philadelphia area to grow the American holly, *Ilex opaca*. It is indigenous. Great masses of this lovely tree are visible in woods along the highways in New Jersey and Delaware. Longwood Gardens, just south of us, have several large holly trees on the terrace of the central conservatory. These trees, which must be forty feet tall, are pruned high enough to allow benches for sitting underneath their dense shade. They stand in the most exposed situation possible and, in the years we've gone to the gardens, have shown no weather damage.

But for the true horticulturist, that's much too easy. It is in our nature to want the challenge that other hollies give us.

We began at the beginning. We bought an American holly and an English one. We put the American on a sunny front terrace, beneath a sheltering pin oak. It thrived. We knew the English holly would need a more protected environment, so we planted it on our house's most northerly side.

That needs a comment. We have what is called an eleven-o'clock house. Most houses are so oriented that if you draw axes through the house, the north-south axis runs from north at noon to south at six o'clock. An eleven-o'clock house's north-south axis runs from eleven to five. This changes the available sunlight a good deal, assuring that plants on the northerly side will, in winter, get no morning sun at all, but will get a lot of late-afternoon sun. We hoped this disposition would suit the English holly. It didn't. The holly lingered and languished and finally died.

Meanwhile, when my mother was inundating us with seedlings of *Elaeagnus pungens*, she was also forwarding a fair number of seedlings that she called Oregon grape holly. This plant had also seized the southern fancy and everyone was growing it.

Oregon grape holly is not, of course, a holly, although its leaves are shaped like holly leaves. When young, they are a light apple green and soft and slightly limp. When winter comes, they turn a reddish brown. The next spring, they turn green again, but this time a dark Lincoln green, and stiff. The blossoms, which appear in May, come in densely clustered gobbets of chrome yellow gathered on their stalks as if they had been squeezed directly from a tube of oil paint. Their shininess gives them the look of expensive jewelry. They mature in September to small blue-black fruit in clusters like small grapes. To birds they must be caviar. They disappear almost at once. The true name of the plant is *Mahonia aquifolium*.

Some books say that *Mahonia aquifolium* is hardy to our zone. Others suggest that this is a marginal hardiness. Not as sensitive as *Elaeagnus pungens*, *M. aquifolium* likes protection from the prevailing winter winds. It likes best the medium shade that occurs at the edge of a wood.

We had to do a good deal of experimenting with our *Mahonia aquifolium* before we managed to get it in optimum places. The first place we tried was behind a forsythia with a southeast exposure. So long as we left it in that arrangement, the late frosts of spring killed it back. We took out the forsythia and replaced it with blue hollies. Ever since, the *M. aquifolium* has prospered. As I look at the arrangement, I would say it gave the grape holly the equivalent of a light lath house exposure.

We put a second *Mahonia* about three yards inside the edge of our wood beside a woodland path. It liked the location.

∾

During the early 1970s, Mimi, in her constant rummaging through horticultural news, came across the first of the blue hollies, Blue Boy and Blue Girl. These seemed the answer to a long-felt urge. Exploring them brought us into touch with rather a wonderful story.

No matter how lovely American holly and its siblings are, *Ilex opaca* has flattish leaves that are light green, and often brown green or yellow green, with berries that veer more toward vermilion than crimson. English holly has leaves that tend toward blue green, are more deeply pointed and slenderer and are twisted and contorted. The berries of the English holly tend to be blood red.

We may have grown fond of the idea of growing English holly because it was so difficult to bring a tree of it to maturity. But it wasn't impossible. One of our neighbors nourished an English holly to twenty feet tall. Perhaps atavism was at work. For English holly, *Ilex aquifolium*, has a long and superstitious history.

The pagans of Europe in the distant past brought sprays of native holly into their dwellings so that the fairy, friendly people of the forest might have a refuge from the frigid winter blasts. Holly was used in pagan rites from Norway to the Mediterranean. During a festival called Saturnalia, in dark December, people gave each other holly branches to betoken friendship. By the sixteenth century, every house, church, street corner and market cross was decorated with holly. And all of this would have been English holly.

Most of our original East Coast colonists, having come from England or English influence, nourished a strong reverence for the English holly that the American species, *Ilex opaca*, could stimulate but not entirely satisfy.

Make a rarity of something and you make it infinitely desirable. Among those who developed a strong sense of frustration about English holly was Kathleen K. Meserve. So long as she and her financeer husband, F. Leighton Meserve, lived in New York City, horticulture to Mrs. Meserve was the florist at the corner. Sensing, however, that World War II would bring shortages a farm might fill, the Meserves rented a ten-acre rural establishment on Long Island.

"Do anything with it you like," the owner said, "except bring a cow into the dining room."

Soon Kathleen Meserve was growing and preserving every vegetable the family ate. Her Victory Garden, as such plots were called, was interesting as education, but not so fascinating that she couldn't drop it with great relief as soon as the war ended.

The horticulture bug had bitten her enough, however, to draw her to a lecture on hollies soon after the war. In those days cultivating hollies did not quicken the pulse of horticulturists the way growing irises did or peonies or dahlias. And yet that lecture stimulated her to join the American Holly Society and to look into the subject of hollies.

It was a shame, she thought, that we had no equivalent of the English holly that could survive our winters. It was also a shame that there was no holly dwarfed enough to replace privet or box as foundation plantings for rose gardens.

Kathleen Meserve began collecting hollies that looked promising. She grew them and studied their natures. When local nurseries couldn't supply a species she wanted, she wrote to Henry Hohman, a well-known hybridizer, who did supply the plants.

There are two ways to reproduce many flowers and shrubs, among them, holly. One way is to plant seeds. The other is to root cuttings. Because flowers are vulnerable to random pollinization, a kind of botanical rape, plants from seeds are likely to differ from the parent. But rooted cuttings always come true. To perform such asexual reproduction, one needs a hothouse, because an ideal time to root cuttings is in winter. Kathleen Meserve met this need by making a Wardian Case for her window. The first time she managed to root a cutting, she was so excited she gave a cocktail party to celebrate.

Rooting cuttings was the easy part. Cross pollination took her into the realm of endless variables, beginning with the fact that hollies, being dioe-cious, bear male and female blossoms on different plants. Not only are the sexes separate, they don't bloom at the same time. Nonsynchronized blooming is particularly likely in hollies of different species. Even when a cross is accomplished by collecting pollen and holding it, so many genetic recombinations are possible that no one can predict the outcome of any one cross. Finally, some crosses are improbable, if not impossible, because different hollies have different chromosome numbers. *Ilex aquifolium*, with forty chromosomes, is not likely to cross with *I. opaca*, which has only thirty-six.

❧

It would not be surprising for a leading university to justify large expenditures on such a program of holly hybridizing without any startling results and look askance at a program like Kathleen Meserve's, which had a budget of $15. The secret was that holly crossing was a labor-intensive activity, and Mrs. Meserve supplied all of her labor at no charge.

Endlessly she crossed holly in her kitchen, harvested the seeds, ger-minated them in sphagnum moss and planted them in an outdoor plot. Hybridizing was slow going. Hollies took almost eighteen months to ger-minate.

Among the hollies she chose for hybridizing was *Ilex rugosa*, a small, prostrate shrub that grows on the mountains of northern Japan and looks somewhat like a spreading euonymus. She chose it for its winter hardi-ness and its tendency to be a runt.

The first few winters that Mrs. Meserve lined out her holly plants were mild. Everything thrived. Then came the inevitable hard winter with sustained low temperatures below zero and sudden freezes and thaws: the kind of weather that plays havoc with broad-leaved evergreens. When Mrs. Meserve looked out that spring, all she could see was brown, brown, brown. Four or five years of hard work down the drain. Hopelessly she plodded through the ruins. And stopped. Was it possible? Did she see some green here and there?

Yes she did! But what was it? She had, as it turned out, males and females of a holly that tended to be dwarf, looked like English holly but was hardy to very low temperatures. The cross was *Ilex aquifolium* with *Ilex rugosa*. If the cross could be kept true, these could be very important hollies.

Kathleen Meserve took the surviving plants through a rigorous program of asexual reproduction. She named these hollies Blue Boy and Blue Girl, patented them and, through Jackson and Perkins, introduced them in 1964. The Arnold Arboretum designated these hollies a new botanical species and named it *meserveae* after its discoverer. All further crosses were called *Ilex × meserveae*.

After Charles Perkins, the Jackson and Perkins partner who had bought the rights to the hollies, died, Mrs. Meserve moved her patent and the management of her hollies to Conard-Pyle of West Grove, Pennsylvania. With their encouragement, she continued to develop new hollies. Blue Prince, introduced in 1972, is truly ornamental and grows to fifteen feet. Blue Princess, which followed in 1973, is a twelve- to fifteenfoot mate for Blue Prince. Finally, in that same year, Mrs. Meserve achieved in Blue Angel one of the hollies that had been her goal. Blue Angel grows no higher than six to eight feet, has foliage like a miniature English holly, is hardy to twenty below and provides a wonderful foundation planting. Blue Maid, introduced in 1979, is the largest of the blue hollies, higher than fifteen feet. Blue Stallion, a male with smooth leaves, blooms all season and ensures good pollination for all the females.

Mimi bought the blue hollies steadily, putting them wherever she needed a foundation planting or a living screen. We now have a Blue Boy, about six Blue Girls and fifteen or so Blue Princesses. The single male seems to provide enough pollen for all, judging by the results, for they are all loaded with berries. Though these shrubs grow faster than box, they are still slow growers. They tend to grow thicker more rapidly than they grow taller. Our oldest one, a Blue Girl, now about fourteen years old, is five feet high and five feet through. This echoes its *Ilex rugosa* ancestor, which tends to be a low, spreading plant.

What is nice about the spreading is that we always have plenty of holly to trim at Christmas without seriously altering the looks of our plants, and all of this holly has the dark, blue-green, contorted leaves of English holly and its blood red berries. We can bring it in for the fairy, friendly people of our forest.

The Southern Connection

With eleagnus and holly the minicli-
mate played a partial role. But with the southern magnolia, *Magnolia
grandiflora*, a miniclimate was essential. No miniclimate, no magnolia.

Why bother with such a tree? Well, as a southerner, it was in my blood
to cherish the southern magnolia. When I was growing up in Atlanta, my
friends and I got a lot of innocent merriment from novels by northern
authors in which heroines wore magnolias in their hair. Living where magnolias were the small-flowered *Magnolia denudata* from China or M. *obovata* from Japan, these authors evidently supposed a magnolia blossom was
about the size of a gardenia.

To a southerner, however, the name *magnolia* conjures up the *Magnolia grandiflora* and no other. The blossom of this deliciously lovely tree is
eight inches in diameter. There is even a variety called 'Gloriosa' with a
twelve-inch flower. One of these flowers in a heroine's hair would conceal her as effectively as a parasol. From the weight standpoint, she would
be more comfortable wearing half of a Rocky Ford cantaloupe.

But a heroine strong enough and courageous enough to dare wearing a magnolia would walk in a cloud of the most renowned southern fragrance. The blossom of *Magnolia grandiflora* emits a wonderful perfume: heavy and rich, partaking of lemons and melons with hints of clove or cinnamon. Alas. Unlike the flowers of M. *denudata* and M. *obovata*, the blossom of the grandiflora lives a brief life—no more than twenty-four hours.

Throughout the coastal South, from Virginia to Texas, the *Magnolia grandiflora* is commonplace. When I visited Atlanta in 1993, I saw few houses without one. These great trees, rising eighty to a hundred feet, rattling in the wind like wooden jalousies, dot the edges of lawns and the marges of drives. They are such dense umbrellas that if you crawled under one on the brightest summer day, you would be in almost total darkness. If you hid under one in a storm, you might get struck by lightning, but you wouldn't get wet. Magnolia leaves, glossy, heavy and convex, overlap like shingles and point downward to shoot water off to the sides.

∽

Anyone who has truly known *Magnolia grandiflora* yearns to have one about. So I yearned, although most gardening books warned that this tree was not reliably hardy above zone 7. In our zone 6, the harsh winds and chills of winter would kill this delicate tree.

We accepted this gospel until Longwood Gardens completed their rock garden. Its upper path, which circled to the bridge across the falls, must have been a good fifty feet above the pond. Looking down from this path, one looked into the top of a semicircle of *Magnolia grandiflora*. All of these trees flourished, and from early June until well into September, all were enriched with magnificent flowers: white with a suggestion of cream when they first opened, taking on a yellowish tinge as the day progressed. The upper walk was planted heavily with several varieties of pines. These, plus the wall that supported the walk, screened the magnolias from northeast, north and east winds and from all winter sun save the afternoon sun from the southwest.

This arrangement agreed with that called for in the fifth printing, 1973, of the Brooklyn Botanic Garden's *Three Hundred Finest Trees and*

Shrubs for Temperate Climates, which said that *Magnolia grandiflora* could be raised in zone 6 as individual specimens in sheltered locations, provided they were given reasonably full winter shade.

From the moment Mimi and I noticed and admired the Longwood magnolias, we itched to try one of our own. My sister in Atlanta had on her house espaliered magnolias that displayed the flowers like some strange, exotic fruit. The arrangement suggested two situations at our house where the magnolias might grow. On a trip to Atlanta, we bought two eighteen-inch magnolia saplings and brought them home.

We knew that the two locations we had selected had miniclimates, but were they what magnolia wished? One lay in a chimney angle on the west side of the house. It got little winter wind and had winter sun only in the last hour or so before sunset; the other lay in the angle behind our American holly, was absolutely protected from winter wind and was overhung by a pin oak, but was open to winter sun from noon until dusk.

The tree in the first location grew more rapidly than the tree in the second and bloomed first. But it had no such lath house effect as the pin oak gave. Severe winters killed it back. It kept trying to return from the roots, but the cold browned it each year until it died.

ℬ

Unlike *Magnolia denudata* and M. *obovata*, both of which are well known in the Northeast, but both of which are deciduous, M. *grandiflora* is an evergreen. Its leaves, glossy as green patent leather, appear, even in winter's cold, to continue some essential photosynthesis. The old leaves don't turn brown and drop until new spring growth is well advanced. Also, these leaves, which turn first yellow and then brown, remain firmly fixed until the last of their green disappears. This tends to confirm their winter role as nourishers. Winters cold enough to brown out all or most of a magnolia's leaves will kill the tree, if they come too often. Our tree has survived several occasions of two harsh winters back to back, but not without visible damage.

The magnolia we planted in the angle with more sunny hours but with the protection of the oak is still with us. More than twenty-five years old and thirty feet tall, it has produced as many as fifty blossoms in a season. After blossoms fade, its petals fall in twists of russet suede and the cones form and mature.

Magnolia cones are more like small pineapples than pinecones. As they grow, their color changes from apple green to bright yellow to the russet suede look and finally to a greenish black. Between the russet suede and the greenish black stages, the cones commence to disgorge scarlet seeds the size of grains of corn. If you crush these seeds, you will produce an intense, highly spiced magnolia fragrance.

New magnolias can be raised from these seeds, but the process is complicated. The directions Bernard McMahon gives in his *American Gardener* say this:

> The seeds of the different kinds of magnolia should be
> sown immediately after being ripe, or be preserved in damp
> sand or earth until March; for, if kept dry until that time,
> very few or any will vegetate until the year following; and
> indeed may not until the second season, even if sown when
> ripe. They may also be propagated by layers and suckers
> and by grafting and budding upon one another.

Mimi's method for germinating the seeds of *Magnolia grandiflora* was to store them in the refrigerator for five to six months in plastic bags full of peat moss and then to plant them. That may be excessive chilling, but it gave good results.

Other names for *Magnolia grandiflora* are the bull bay or evergreen magnolia. There are ten genera and about a hundred species in the family Magnoliaceae. The most prevalent member of the family in the East is *Liriodendron tulipifera*, the tulip tree or tulip poplar. Paul Hamlyn, in his *Pictorial Encyclopaedia of Plants and Flowers*, says: "Many botanists believe these trees are one of the most primitive of existing families of flowering plants."

❧

Apart from its susceptibility to being done in by a hard winter's cold, *Magnolia grandiflora*, with its great leaves dark and dense all winter, is vulnerable to ice and snow. Ice storms can build enormous weight on the leaves and break branches and limbs. Snow may also stick to the leaves, but if there is wind while the snow is dry, the snow will shake out of the tree.

Fortunately, the limbs and branches of *Magnolia grandifolia* are supple. They can take considerable weight without breaking and usually will recover their original posture. I've seen parts of our magnolia, bent forty degrees with ice, recover their original shape entirely by the end of the following summer. The chief forces of winter that damage the magnolia are chill, drying winds and the winter sun striking frozen leaves early in the day. These forces seem worse when they come at the end of the season. When we have sudden deep freezes in late February or in March, we can expect to see every magnolia leaf turn brown and fall before the middle of May. When no late freezes occur, the heavy, crisp brown leaves tumble down slowly until near the end of June, when the new foliage is out and the tree is blooming.

In a way, the leaves are nuisances. They are heavy, stiff as tiles and have a lot of bulk. Fortunately they are quite brittle. A rotary mower will churn them into coarse flakes.

Any who have known the southern magnolia miss it in other climes and long to see it again. One illustrious American longed for it in France. In 1786, Thomas Jefferson sent these words from Paris to Dr. David Ramsey in Charleston:

> ...a person whom I am very desirous of obliging has asked
> me to procure...some plants of the Magnolia grandiflora...
> if you can be instrumental in procuring them, you will
> gratify me much.

Three Special Trees

Chairs and tables are the furniture of a house; trees and shrubs are the furniture of a garden. Where natural trees have grown to be specimens, we plan our gardens around them, shaping walks and streams to display these trees to their best advantage.

Most trees grow in groves, where the nearness of other trees misshapes and compresses them. A true specimen usually stands alone upon a hill or in a pasture or a marsh. There is an old saying that to achieve full and complete development of individuality, a tree or a person must grow uncrowded and in the open. It becomes harder and harder for this to happen to either.

Those who design gardens make up for the shortage of specimens by bringing in unusual trees intended to contribute to the design. Mimi planted three such species: paper birch, *Betula papyrifera*; the Chinese scholar tree, *Sophora japonica*; and yellowwood, *Cladrastis lutea*. She developed her fancy for each in a different way.

Paper birch grew abundantly in New England when Hiawatha was making his birchbark canoes. The paper birch grows well in Pennsylvania, but it is not the birch that shows white trunks along roads and railroads in eastern Pennsylvania and New Jersey. That birch, *Betula populifolia*, the white or gray birch, is a fragile and short-lived tree that grows no taller than twenty to thirty feet. If we ever had much paper birch in Pennsylvania, it all got lumbered out years ago.

Mimi's conviction was that we must plant lots of paper birches. Mimi liked them because of their beauty and their ability to live a long time. She always planted them in clumps of three or five. Her sense of style insisted the number should be odd. The first clump Mimi tried had three trees, planted close together. A storm snapped off one of these so that clump became an unstylish twosome. To avoid another small clump, the next time Mimi planted five saplings at the end of our ha-ha wall. One of our sons broke off a sapling while riding a sled over the wall, leaving a clump of four. In disgust, Mimi planted four birches in her third and final clump. Another son, on an out-of-control mower, removed one of the four and left Mimi finally with a three-tree birch planting.

Until they got to be five or six years old, the paper birches didn't look like much. They had a dark brown bark flecked with short strokes of lighter brown. They bloomed before they came into leaf, the blooms being long—about three-inch—yellow catkins. The leaves that followed were a brilliant, tender light green and looked pleated.

At a certain point in maturing, the brown bark peels away to reveal a light beige underbark with horizontal light brown stripes called lenticels. On being exposed to air, this bark turns white. As it ages, it grows chalky. Rubbing it chalks the hand as a used blackboard does. From this point on, the tree molts some bark each year, occasionally in sheets a foot long and a foot wide. Although the normal inclination of the bark is to fritter off in narrow strips, with care one can peel off sheets larger than a foot square. The Indians and early settlers knew that birch bark, peeled away carefully, trimmed and flattened, made excellent writing paper. Our youngest son, while courting his wife-to-be, sent her letters written on birch bark.

Paper birch will grow seventy to eighty feet high, and our first planting has nearly reached seventy feet. The new limbs the trees put out in the process were initially brown. In their second year, they turned white from the trunk outward, always maintaining one or two feet of brown at their ends. As is typical of many of our native trees, like the tulip poplar, the lower limbs of birches tend to die and break away to leave long, straight trunks of marred bark. The wood of the fallen limbs rots to pulp very quickly. But the bark does not. It contains a resin that makes it waterproof.

The paper birch added unexpected columns of white to our landscape. Against winter snows the trees have a ghostly look, as if they are a part of the snow. In spring and summer, their white glows in startling contrast to the greens, blacks and browns of other trees. For obvious reasons many artists like to include paper birches in their landscapes.

ॐ

The second tree Mimi chose she found on a visit to Longwood Gardens. We used, regularly, to go plant shopping at Longwood. We would rummage among the Longwood goodies, like a dowager going at a box of bonbons, and select new plants to try, new trees to plant. Then Mimi would search catalogues for them.

One humid August afternoon, as we wandered beneath some trees on the path to the Italian gardens, we realized, suddenly, that we were amid a sound that was heavy, ominous and roughly similar to a light plane revving up. The pulsating hum and throb was so startling that other visitors edged away.

Our instinct, as always, was to explore before running. The instinct may one day be the death of us but meanwhile we won't miss much. We saw that the air was full of honeybees. They were not being drawn by flowers at ground level but by something in several tall trees that loomed above us.

To learn what could be in several sixty-foot trees in August that would lure honeybees at almost swarming density, we backed away to get a distant view. To our astonishment, we saw that the trees were in full bloom. The blossoms were tightly clustered bunches of what looked like small sweet peas. They were a greenish white.

The label in the fork of one trunk said:

SCHOLAR TREE
Sophora japonica

Mimi needed more than a year to find a catalogue that offered *Sophora japonica* saplings. The catalogue was loquacious about the beauty and appeal of the tree but vague about its preferences in soil, exposure, feeding and sunlight. No matter. We ordered one.

The Bush-Browns, from whom we took most of our early guidance, advised that *Sophora* liked rich soil and wished to be protected from winds. Its common name was Chinese scholar tree. Most sources agreed that the tree originated in China, and everybody said it could grow to eighty feet, a fact that ought to govern placement even if the planter wasn't likely to be around to view the ultimate majesty.

Trust the Japanese to get into the act. Although introduced into England about two hundred years ago, the scholar tree didn't grow popular until after World War II. As soon as it grew popular, it began to be called the Japanese pagoda tree, hence *japonica* instead of *sinensis*. It is astonishing how many plants that actually originated somewhere else, usually in China, are *japonica* owing to the zeal of the Japanese.

The *Pictorial Encyclopaedia of Plants and Flowers*, by Paul Hamlyn, told us that *Sophora japonica* was a member of the pea family, Leguminosae. This accounted for the pealike blossoms and, according to Hamlyn's pictures, its fruit, which looked like strings of yellow-green, bean-shaped beads.

Taylor's Garden Guide called *Sophora* the latest blooming of all flowering trees and set its blooming time as mid-August, which was when we had seen it at Longwood ablaze with flowers, abuzz with bees. *Sophora*, Taylor went on, was hardy as far north as Boston. *The Encyclopaedia of Trees, Shrubs, Vines and Lawns*, spurning the rich-soil dictum, said the tree would survive in well-drained, sandy loam that varied from moist to dry. But don't plant it near paved walks, another source cautioned. The falling fruit, when crushed, is very slippery. The *Brooklyn Botanic Garden*

Record was the source that really came to grips with the problem: "*Sophora* grows well under almost any conditions, including poor, rocky, dry soils. It withstands city and seacoast conditions and is comparatively free from pests and disease."

Brooklyn could not have foreseen the pest we inadvertently visited on our *Sophora*. We planted our sapling in a stretch of recent fill that we were trying to convert to lawn. It attracted the attention of our Irish setter. Each time a few leaves came out, the setter would stand thoughtfully and chew them off, rather like an old man picking his teeth.

Not because we ever expected to have a sixty-foot, bee-gorged miracle, but out of compassion, we girded our *Sophora* with a cylinder of page wire to keep the setter at bay. Despite the setter and the soil in which we had planted it, hardpan enriched with boulders, our scholar tree survived.

Presently, we broadened our terrace to leave the *Sophora* at stage center. By then, the tree had grown to six feet and had fans of light, delicate leaves, like the leaves of the honey locust, *Gleditsia triacanthos*, whose relative it is.

Would it ever bloom?

Not until it reached twenty feet. We noticed, in July of the year it achieved this height, small racemes of lightish green punctuating the darker sprays of leaves. These clusters proved to be buds. They kept growing and spreading the way lilac buds do, but they bloomed in loose terminal panicles instead of the lilac's pyramidal panicles. They reminded us of wisteria.

The buds developed so fast at first that we expected them to bloom in late July. Instead, they needed four weeks from the first suggestion of buds' forming to mature to a final flowering. Not until the morning of the fifteenth of August did we see our first blooms. They were so small and their white so tinged with green that we couldn't be sure until we went very close.

As is typical of blooming panicles, the scholar tree started blooming at the stem end and slowly bloomed to the tip, shedding early blossoms before forming the later ones. The process took another three weeks. All the while a gentle rain of greenish white sifted down beneath the tree.

And I found it pleasant to fancy that Chinese scholars had stood, pensive, in other such rains of delicate blossoms, absorbing some special benison from a tree whose processes were as deliberate, subtle and perfected as the philosophy of Lao-tse, as typified in this observation:

> The prudent man avoids all appearance of suspicion;
> He does not adjust his hat under a plum tree,
> Nor in a melon patch pull up his socks;
> Moderate your brilliance and difficulties will disappear.

Seen from our terrace, the upper tree was an ethereal cloud of pale chartreuse. A light sweet-pea fragrance filled the air. As the tree stood between us and the prevailing summer winds, it bathed us with waves of scent, like castile soap in a warm shower. Our concentration of honeybees was not as great as at Longwood, but masses of bumblebees, butterflies and other pollinating insects swarmed around.

We were jubilant. We were always jubilant when we more or less matched something Longwood had done. Now we had a tree that would blossom beautifully each August. We thought.

Not so. The next August it had only a few panicles. It turned out to bloom vigorously only in alternate years, as the trees of Yellow Delicious apples do.

The *Sophora* puts out a good deal of tentative growth in the form of small twigs that spring, like porcupine quills, in all directions from limbs and trunk. Most of this growth, especially the part that comes after the middle of July, dies when winter arrives. Much of it can be brushed off.

The natural shape of *Sophora*, according to our sources, is spreading. A spreading eighty-foot tree should be enough shade for a convention of scholars, and a pretty sight that would be, but such a spread in the middle of our terrace would have obliterated our view. To get something taller and slenderer than the standard configuration, we did some pruning. We took the precaution of pruning in the dead of winter, in case *Sophora* should be a bleeder.

Our precaution was in vain. *Sophora* was not a bleeder, but the next summer, its summer for a heavy bloom, our tree sulked. Not only did it not bloom, it came only thinly and sparsely to leaf. We were distraught. We had killed our tree!

The next year we watched anxiously. Would it leaf, or would it stand a gaunt, dead, twenty-foot monument to our rashness? Came May. Light, almost yellow tendrils appeared. By June the foliage was as plentiful as ever. August brought a light bloom.

Now a sixty-foot beauty, our *Sophora* blooms so densely that the leaves themselves disappear. For three weeks in August a blizzard of chartreuse blossoms descends. Then the fruit forms: thousands of strings of yellow-green beans, the tree looking more fully in bloom with the fruit than with the blossoms. The leaves fall after the first hard frost. Most of the fruit hangs and holds its color until the next spring, gradually turning yellow brown, then dark brown. The following March and April, about half of these seeds remain on the tree.

ॐ

Although *Sophora* was not a bleeder, the next specimen Mimi planted, *Cladrastis lutea*, was. Yellowwood was also, when in bloom, an exquisitely beautiful sight, particularly where we planted it, near our Father Hugo roses. These yellow roses bloomed at the same time as the yellowwood.

Mimi was drawn to this tree for the same reason she was later drawn to the *Franklinia*. It was a tree found only in a limited place. The original *Cladrastis* was native to a small region of limestone cliffs in Kentucky, North Carolina and eastern Tennessee. It had a smooth, gray-black bark, like some of the beeches.

After she had found and ordered a *Cladrastis lutea*, Mimi saw a really huge specimen in the gardens of John Bartram. She followed with helpless rage the fate of a grove of old yellowwoods that the University of Pennsylvania destroyed to make way for a parking lot. Not even heavy picketing could prevent the destruction.

One of the novel things we learned about this tree during the first ten years we had it was its capacity for bleeding. It simply could not be pruned at any time except in the dead of winter, when the temperature was below freezing. Even then, the cut would drool an icicle. Trim a limb at any other time, and the cut ran like a faucet.

Because Mimi planted our *Cladrastis lutea* at the side of the terrace, where the Tipsy Virgin consorted with Napoleon's Hat, we didn't watch it closely. We were aware of it, when the roses bloomed, as a rising tree that spread its arms wide. During all of this long time, if a blossom or two appeared, we missed it.

Then came the year it bloomed, and it was incredible. Even more than the *Sophora*, this tree had blossoms like wisteria. The blooming panicles hung three to four inches apart, with a larger mass of blossoms at the top, so that each panicle had the silhouette of a small white angel with wings. Because of the way the limbs spread, like arms thrust far apart, many of the panicles seemed to float in the air without support. Each panicle was twelve to fourteen inches long and its white blossoms were unusually brilliant. The fragrance beneath the tree was a mixture of lilacs and pinks and was very heavy. As with the *Sophora*, the blossoms were dense enough to obscure the foliage. When we looked up through the tree we could think: Heaven must look like this.

I suspect that our *Cladrastis lutea* is not planted in ideal soil and lacks enough lime because it has bloomed prolifically only twice and bloomed noticeably only four or five times. One year, when I have the time, I will run a test to see whether lime improves the blooming.

We have planted other specimen trees that have prospered to varying extents, for Mimi loves to try new tree experiments, but no other trees have been so spectacular as these three.

WILDLIFE

The Summer of Hubert

Having enough money to add a wing and, two years later, a swimming pool did not mean we were rich enough to stop doing a lot of jobs ourselves or that we had now mewed up our sons in an elegant keep that insulated them from nature. Our sons, particularly Chris, our youngest, ranged the wood, exploring the dens and lairs of red foxes, woodchucks, muskrats, rabbits, field mice, possums and skunks, reminding us that there was more to country living than horticulture. There were also wild animals.

Chris was forever bringing injured animal babies to be nursed back to health. We discouraged such activity. It was cruel to make a pet of a wild animal that presently would have to be released. Also, nursing wild babies usually didn't save them. They lasted long enough to make a home in our hearts, then died. But Chris was so earnest about animals, he overthrew our better judgment much too often. This probably made us receptive to Hubert.

It began on a June Saturday. The air was quick with the beginning of summer. I came out onto the side terrace, intending to mow the front field. Chris and Rip Carthcart, from across the road, were staring up into the black walnut tree that stood beside the house. A dark shape dropped to Rip's head and let out a challenging squawk.

It was a crow.

I walked toward Rip. The crow, with wings the size of bath towels, flapped back up to the limb of the walnut and set up a great racket of cawing and clicking and scratching his head with his foot. He sounded like a noisy shortstop giving his team the word.

"His name is Hubert," Rip said.

"Won't he fly away?" Chris asked.

Rip shook his head. "The problem is to make him stay away."

Hubert dropped to Chris's shoulder. It was a bit like being landed on by a light plane. Very loudly into Chris's ear Hubert said: "Tock, tock, tock!"

All of my feelings against adopting a wild animal rose in me. You destroyed its other options. When you did that, you were obligated to take care of the animal for life.

The sight of this pet crow named Hubert made me sad. Rip was a kind and attentive boy, blond and tall and skinny, but his mother was given to fads and to talking Rip from one fad to another. She had found pet crows in a farmer's market. It would be nice for Rip to have one. He would enjoy it. Next week she would find something else and persuade Rip to forget Hubert. Knowing Chris, I knew we would inherit Hubert.

Chris and Rip walked around to our swimming pool. Hubert circled the house, swooped to the top of the umbrella over the table on the terrace and rattled out a steady line of infield chatter, turning his head this way and that, mouth open, like a radar dish tracking planes.

Hubert was aggressive and fearless. We had a large, fixed tomcat. Hubert attacked him at once, chased him into the yew hedge and came back to the table, saying, "Tock, tock, tock!" with great satisfaction.

Mimi came out. She was enthralled with Hubert. Hubert liked people to be enthralled. He flew under the umbrella and sat on Mimi's shoulder. She whispered to him. Hubert was fascinated. He put his ear to her mouth, opened his beak wide, panted, listened to some more, chattered at her, then told her: "Tock, tock, tock!"

He walked up her arm, looked down from her shoulder and discovered a pack of cigarettes in the pocket of her blouse. He plucked out a cigarette and flew with it to the top of the pool house. He held the cigarette in his mouth as if he were smoking it. Then he put it down and, like a missionary stamping out vice, he pecked it to pieces.

From then on, Hubert came every day. At first he came with Rip. Then he came alone. He found the window of Chris's room and sat on the sill and pecked the screen until Chris got up. That chore done, he flew to the umbrella table on the terrace.

He liked adults better than children. He perched on the table, where Mimi sat to sew, and meddled with everything. He pecked at her sewing and knocked ashtrays to the ground. He stole dimes, quarters, earrings, thimbles—anything that was small and shiny—and hid them under the split cedar shakes of the pool house roof.

He attacked our two dogs and drove them down the lane. The dogs didn't know what to make of something that swooped suddenly from out of nowhere, like an aircraft on a bombing run, and spiked them with a sharp beak.

Hubert showed no interest in other crows. Our countryside teemed with crows. They flapped about in all directions, braying and squawking, holding in our fields large noisy Baptist conventions. But whether he flew over them or under them, Hubert paid the other crows no heed, and they ignored him. Smaller birds, which chased owls, falcons, hawks and other crows, didn't bother Hubert, either. They sensed that he was harmless.

Mimi liked to watch Hubert. She laughed at him. No matter what he did, no matter how outrageous, she laughed. She thought Hubert was cute. Hubert thought Hubert was cute, too.

Once Mimi discovered how Hubert liked to be whispered to, she whispered to him regularly. He would sit very still and listen and look at her, mouth wide open as if he couldn't believe what she told him. Presently he would say to her indignantly: "Tock, tock, tock!" as if urging her, "Speak up! Speak up!" While he did this, he stole a cigarette from her pocket and pecked it to pieces. She pretended fury and threatened him with a fly swatter.

Hubert, his mouth gaping in amazement, backed away. He screamed hurt and outrage and flew to a tree. He stayed for about two minutes, then came back. Mimi forgave him. She said he was like a very bright two-year-old with an attention span of thirty seconds.

∾

One morning Hubert discovered that I ate breakfast at the umbrella table. Well! That really was too good!

While Mimi fixed breakfast, I read a book and drank a cup of coffee. Hubert, one feather sticking out of his head like a cowlick, watched me read and stalked about, muttering. He pecked my book. I closed the book and stared at him. He sidled away and shifted from one foot to the other. Suddenly, with a look of wild daring, he plunged his beak into my coffee. He screamed in rage. It was hot and bitter! He didn't like it. He flew to the top of the pool house and sat squalling.

When Mimi brought my breakfast, Hubert flew back. He walked around the table, but shrank from my coffee cup. He preened his feathers. I cut a small bite of scrambled egg and put it in front of Hubert. He gorged it and waited for more. When I didn't offer any more, he rushed at me and tried to get the rest of my eggs. He flew to my shoulder, my head, my arm, all the while gurgling through the mouthful of egg he already had. I thought he was funny and gave him another bite of egg. He gorged that and kept fluttering at me until my plate was empty. He flew, then, to a corner of the terrace, disgorged all of the egg and pecked it up little by little.

He followed me when I went to my car to drive to the station and sat on the hood and watched me through the windshield. He pecked at the glass and brayed at me to come out. I turned on the windshield wipers. He watched them, his head going back and forth, like a fan at a tennis match. I drove down the lane. Hubert stayed on the car. When I reached the road, he spread his wings and soared away.

The next morning, Hubert decided to have all of my breakfast. He tried to jump into the middle of the plate; he tried to kick it off the table. He pecked my hands and grabbed for my fork. He knocked my book on the floor, all the while braying and slapping his wings in my face.

I swept my arm and knocked Hubert across the terrace. He surged back. I grabbed him and held him so that he couldn't move his wings. I shook him like a cocktail. He squawked with fright. I held him like a football and rifled him into the air.

Hubert traveled about fifteen yards like a forward pass, floundered, wings beating the air, then straightened out. He gave me a final scream of rage and flew home. He stayed away for three days. When he came back, he roosted high in the walnut tree until I left for town.

༝

Hubert kept his distance until Mimi began painting the front of the house. She began on a Saturday morning in July. The hot sun had dried everything. July flies swirled in the trees. Mimi was high on her ladder, her bucket of paint hanging from an S of wire, her brush in her hand. I was at ground level repairing screens.

A sudden, low "Caw!" of delight shattered the morning. Hubert had arrived in the pin oak from which we hung bird feeders. He filled the air with jeers that sounded like wild laughter. He flew to Mimi's head. He swooped off and returned to the high branches of the oak. He dropped to the top of the ladder. From there he noticed the paint.

He flew to Mimi's shoulder to watch. Then he watched from the ladder again, then from the rim of the paint bucket, then from Mimi's head. All the while he grew more excited. He pecked the brush, spat and nattered and yattered complaints. Presently he decided that what Mimi needed was help. He flew to her hand that held the brush and rode it back and forth.

Hubert began to be splattered and streaked with white paint. White paint did not improve his looks. Where once he had been sleek and black with shiny highlights of blue and purple gloss, he now began to look ratty. He still looked like a crow, but he looked less and less like one.

Mimi came down at midmorning for a cigarette and a glass of ale.

Hubert came with her. He watched her pour the ale. He danced about eagerly and demanded some. He pecked the bottle. Mimi pushed him away. He rushed back and dipped his beak into her glass, tipped his head and let the ale run down his throat.

He looked at Mimi and made a sound: "Ahhhhh!"

He paced back and forth and watched her drink. She got a bowl and poured some ale for him. Hubert watched all of this closely. He drank his ale in dainty sips.

From then on, Hubert shared ale with Mimi each morning. It made him noisy and feisty.

❧

A colony of jays lived in our orchard. One morning a big jay got tired of mauling the other jays, noticed Hubert and screeched his way to the top of the umbrella. He set up a loud jarring racket. He flew at Hubert.

Hubert squared his shoulders, like a drunk shrugging into an overcoat, flapped his wings and went after the jay. We tried to call him back. It was no use. As Hubert followed him, the jay soared high in the air, then plunged at Hubert. The jay tried to drive his beak through Hubert's head. He hit Hubert's neck instead and knocked out three black feathers. We watched them drift to the ground.

Hubert, cawing defiance, landed on a limb in an apple tree in the middle of jay territory. He filled the air with abusive language and loud challenges. Five jays dive-bombed him, all trying to drive a beak into his brain.

Wild crows passed over, raptor wings with feathers like black fingers, and cawed. They recognized Hubert's call, but he was not one of them.

The jays knocked a good many feathers out of Hubert's neck, but they didn't hurt him much. Hubert got in a lucky blow and brought down one jay. The bird fluttered, bleeding, into a clump of sumac. This startled the jays enough to make them retreat high into the neighboring trees. Hubert flew back to the table. He was a mess. He had lost most of his neck feathers and several from his wings. But he had won! He took a long drink of ale and strutted around, braying.

Summer painting was contagious. Rip's family painted their barn red. Someone else painted with green. Hubert supervised painting everywhere and picked up colors until he was a kind of motley on black. He was also drinking too much ale. It made him fly erratically. He would flap his wings and climb very fast, then lose interest, fold his wings and fall like a rock. At the last moment, he would spread his wings, glide to a fence post and sit there, shaking his head. Where once he had flown straight home, now he zigzagged, just missing trees and bushes. For a while, this probably saved his life.

When the jays attacked, the way Hubert flew baffled them. They knew the moves of a sober crow but not those of a drunken one. Still, they managed to hit him often enough to knock out the rest of his neck feathers. His real neck was no thicker than a pencil. His great head looked heavy enough to snap it off. When he spread his wings to fly, gaps appeared where feathers were missing. But Hubert neither noticed nor minded. He blundered on, stupid, willful, stubborn and pleased with himself.

∾

We left for the shore the second week in August. Rip's family went on vacation at the same time. I didn't ask Rip what he would do about Hubert. I shrank from hearing. His mother would never let a crow interfere with a vacation.

The day before we left, I saw Hubert for the last time. He was so covered with paint and dust that not much of his black showed. So many of his feathers were gone that he looked like a tramp in ragged clothes. But his spirit was fine. He was loud and brash and eager for his ale.

When we got home from our vacation, Hubert was gone. Rip, near tears, feeling guilt and the loss of a friend, came to tell us. People said they had seen Hubert—a crow all covered with paint—miles away. Could that be true? And nobody had found a dead crow, covered with paint. Maybe he would come home.

He never did, of course.

What happened to Hubert will always be a mystery. Our countryside has woods and tangled bogs where no one goes for months on end. A dead bird could disappear there in a week and not leave even a trace of feathers.

I fantasized, though, a nobler end for Hubert, a glorious end, an end befitting his stubborn bravado. I pictured him and the jay, circling and plunging at each other, brave aviators in a dogfight high above the valley where our creek runs away.

The willows wear yellow leaves, brilliant in the sunlight against a hard blue sky. The jay is quick and darting; Hubert is big and clumsy. The two of them sweep high, then plunge so low they disappear into the willows. Hubert knocks out some jay feathers and brays in triumph. Flecks of white and blue sift down upon the waters of the creek.

Gradually Hubert tires. His turns grow sluggish, as if he knows he has nowhere to go if he wins. As if he understands that chance, by making him a toy, has made him a victim. He keeps losing the jay, now, keeps flopping about blindly, seeking him.

Twice the jay soars, plunges at Hubert and misses. The third time, his outstretched beak pierces Hubert's skull and sticks there. He and Hubert hang together in the air, flapping wildly, black and blue feathers drifting down. Still tangled, they fall. And the jay learns that to commit murder you often have to commit suicide.

Probably it didn't happen that way, but why not? Why shouldn't a stubborn, silly dispossessed crow have his moment of glory?

A Defense of Bats

A phone call from a tenant in a house we owned focused our attention on bats. The house was full of fleas, said the tenant. The bats in the attic had brought them. He had a thing about those bats. He had complained about them before, as bats, and we had ignored him. The fleas gave him a chance to get righteous and demand that I deal with the problem.

Such a complaint, when strong and loud, tends to unseat judgment. If Mimi and I had stopped to think, we would have realized that bats might generate other problems, but being insect eaters, they would be unlikely to bring in fleas.

Our own attic was full of bats, *Pipistrellus subflavus*, as nearly as we could judge. It had been, ever since we moved in. Many summers the usual visitation of fleas plagued us for a week or ten days, but these infestations could always be traced to our cats. Unless a cat had been there, we never found fleas near the attic.

Stung by the tenant's complaint but trying to be a conscientious landlord, I called several exterminators. None had any idea how to get rid of bats. Most believed it couldn't be done. But to a man, these exterminators were positive about fleas. None had ever heard of bats bringing in fleas. Any place that had fleas had them because dogs or cats had been mewed up in it.

Our tenant had cats. When I confronted him, I learned that he had gone off for a weekend while his wife was away. He had left three cats locked in his house. When he returned, the place was crawling with fleas and he knew his wife would be furious unless he had something to blame them on.

❧

This little adventure dramatizes the bum rap bats have been getting from time immemorial. And bats have been around since time immemorial. Remains of bats from the Upper Eocene epoch, when the orders of mammals arose, closely resemble the bats we have now. Bats haven't changed much.

Bats are closely related to such insectivores as shrews and moles, from which they may have evolved, taking to the air by way of mutations, perhaps with some intervening stage of gliding like flying squirrels.

The end product is the only mammal that has the power of true flight. Its wings are, in effect, webbed arms and hands (hence the name of the order, Chiroptera, meaning hand-wings). Arms and elongated fingers provide the ribs for the wings, which are attached to the body. This arrangement folds like an umbrella and allows the bat to compress itself into a far smaller space than a bird of equal size.

Their extraordinary compressibility lets bats do things that seem supernatural. By flattening out, a bat can slip under doors and through cracks that not even a vole could penetrate, creating the illusion of being able to pass through solid walls. After flying about, looking as large as a robin or a jay, a bat can alight, fold up and disappear. Crumpled like a dead leaf and hanging upside down, the bat is almost invisible. People have an atavistic terror of living animals that create such illusions. The knee-jerk instinct is to weave them into frightening legends.

The appearance of bats does little to soften the fright. The long-tongued bats of Latin America, the epauletted bats of Africa, the greater short-nosed fruit bats of Asia and the gray bats of the United States have faces somewhat like tiny fox terriers and are attractive. Most of the rest of the more than one thousand bat varieties are absolute frights. That the features that curdle their countenances have crucial functions doesn't make them any less ugly.

Most bats have pushed-in noses with large nostrils. The naked bat has a snout like a pig. Many species have huge ears. The tomb bat has elephant ears the size of its head. The ears of large-eared bats are out of proportion to their bodies.

As if all of this were not ugliness enough, many bats compound the mess by having faces that are littered with growths called nose leaf. Nose leaves are fringed flaps with long, fine hairs. The amount of nose leaf and the size of ears govern when the bat flies. Bats with no nose leaf and small ears come out at dusk, fly until full dark and return to roost. As day begins to break, they fly again until full sunrise. Bats with heavy nose leaf and large ears fly in the dead of night. The nose leaf and the ears provide a kind of full-service sonar that operates by echolocation.

A bat's sense of surroundings is so keen, it can perceive objects without actually touching them. While flying, insectivorous bats utter sharp squeaks inaudible to most humans. These bounce off insects and other objects to give the bat locations.

It is an error to suppose, though, that bats have poor eyesight. From type to type, particularly among those that fly at dawn and gloaming, their sight is moderate to good. When there is enough light, they use their eyes, augmented, of course, by the sonar.

∾

Bats are so accommodated to flight that they seldom alight on the ground unless some prey they stalk, some grasshopper or frog or small animal, is there. Their favorite position of repose is hanging head downward by their feet with wings tightly folded. They feed and drink in flight and fish for such prey as small frogs and salamanders, and mate in flight. The females carry their young in flight, clinging to their bodies.

Most bats bear only one young, although a few species bear two or three. The gestation period ranges from forty days to eight months, depending upon body size, but females don't always breed every year, so the replacement of bat population is slow compared with replacement among other mammals of similar size. The fact that as many as 75 percent of the young of some species perish contributes to this slowness. On the other hand, bats are long-lived for their size. The oldest wild bat recorded lived to be thirty, and many twenty-year-olds have been noted.

Bats either migrate or hibernate. Those in our attic—we must have had a constant population of around three hundred for years—migrate in September and return in early March.

So far as we could tell, except in breeding season, the sexes lived separately. The bats had two entrances to our attic, one on each side of the house. As the attic was not partitioned, we like to think that each sex had its own exit.

Every evening in good weather, at about sundown, we watched the stream of bats drop out of our eaves, like a shower of black beanbags, and fly, crazy, topsy-turvying, into the gloaming. Or as Lewis Carroll put it:

> Twinkle, twinkle, little bat,
> How I wonder what you're at.
> Up above the world you fly
> Like a teatray in the sky.

As I explored bats, I was surprised to learn that a bat is not a rodent. I had been misled by a song in a Walt Disney short about a mouse who yearned to fly, got some wings by magic and tried to join a colony of bats. The bats disapproved and told him he was nothing but a nothing, not a bat and no longer a mouse, not a thing at all.

My misapprehension of a bat's being a rodent grew out of a useful function that I thought it must be a rodent to accomplish. I had always understood that two types of rodents would not inhabit the same place. If you had mice, for instance, you wouldn't have rats or chipmunks or squirrels.

The most important place to keep cleared of mice or chipmunks or squirrels is an attic. Most house fires that begin in attics—and that's where a good half of them begin—are caused by a rodent's building a nest of fur, shavings and other tinder on and around electric wires and wearing away insulation until a spark, or wires overheated by a short circuit, ignite the tinder. If our bats were rodents, I deduced, they would keep other rodents out.

They kept other rodents out without being rodents. They also dislodged a beehive. For years we had bees in an eave. Gradually the bats must have worked their way to the hive. One autumn our terrace was littered with dead bees. The next year, a fresh swarm tried to recapture the old place, failed and had to settle for building a hive outside on the soffit.

ⱷ

Because I have come to like our bats and to consider them a kind of fire brigade, I have reflected on how they got such a bad image. From literature and legend, I suspect. Back in the days when midnight was still a mysterious and a witching hour, Hallowe'en always mixed bats in with witches, black cats, owls and other denizens of darkness. Bram Stoker had in 1897 published his book, *Dracula*, about a vampire who traveled at night in the form of a giant bat. Stoker was probably inspired by the fact that when he was writing, vampire bats had recently been identified. After the first *Dracula* movie appeared in 1931 and dramatized the idea of bats as vampires, everybody was sure all bats were vampires.

Such nonsense!

The few existing vampire bats live only in the West Indies, Central and South America. They endure only in hot climates. They could never survive where Dracula lived, in the northwest Rumanian area called Transylvania.

Far from being a huge animal that could be a transformed human, the vampire bat is small, no larger than three inches. Its bite is also small. Being bitten by one—if one is bitten, for they prefer animal blood—would not be much worse than being bitten by a large mosquito or a deer fly. Few vampire bats are exclusively bloodsuckers; most also eat considerable fruit.

But Charles Darwin had reported in *The Voyage of HMS Beagle*, published in 1840, that his servant had seen a *Desmodus* bat sucking blood from the withers of a camp horse. That was enough for Bram Stoker and, later, for the public.

Such horror legends appealed to the public love of *frisson*, but they alone would not have sustained the hate campaign without the collateral repulsions of these animals' ugliness, erratic movement and clustering life-style.

Because it pursues insects at night, a bat flies a darting, zigzag course instead of the graceful, predictable flight of a swallow, which does the same job by day. Indoors, this kind of flight becomes terrifying. Women will go into hysterics much faster at a bat in the air than at a mouse on the floor. A chief reason is that bats tend to fly into a woman's hair. The bat doesn't do this maliciously. The bat can't help it. The bat's cries, bouncing from hard surfaces, say to its sense of echolocation: here is a wall; here is a table. A head of hair, especially a bouffant hairdo, looks to echolocation like an open door, a hole or an exit. The bat, frantic to escape, flies toward it. Putting on a hat or cap will keep the bat away.

I've proven the way this works many times by driving an errant bat into a closed room and putting in a cat. Within less than a minute the cat, without moving, without at first even being aware of the bat, will have caught and killed it. How? To echolocation, the cat's soft fur registers as an exit, and the bat flies to it.

Despite the views of the exterminators I questioned, bats can be gotten rid of. A geologist told me that he had cleared a cave of bats by stringing two vertical piano wires tautly in the flight path. The bats left because they were colliding with something they couldn't detect. In a house, locating all of the bat exits, waiting until the bats are out and closing the exits will do the job.

But wait! You may decide to keep your bats and encourage them.

One gray bat can eat as many as three thousand flying insects in a night. A colony of free-tailed bats in Texas knocks off two hundred and fifty thousand *pounds* of insects every evening. Our own bats keep us substantially free of mosquitoes, although we have plenty of swamps and pools of standing water where they can breed.

Fruit-eating bats of the tropics are known to pollinate and scatter the seeds of bananas, plantains, dates, mangoes, cashews, breadfruits and figs as well as those of the giant baobab trees and of the iroko tree, which produces valuable timber. We don't know our own bats well enough to know what they may pollinate and sow, but we may be sure they have a horticultural importance, if so many of their fellow species in other parts of the world do. One may have a fondness for frogs, salamanders and grasshoppers, but one might have less enthusiasm for them if bats did not keep their populations in check.

∾

A recent indictment against bats has been that they have and distribute rabies. An absolute lie. Over the past thirty years bats have caused only nine cases of human rabies. The dog population, which no one suggests exterminating, has transmitted many times this number. Among bats, rabies incidence runs less than one half of one percent. Each year thousands of people explore caves populated with huge numbers of bats. No one gets bitten. Healthy bats don't bite people.

Fortunately, today, instead of pumping shotgun fire into flights of bats, as people did in the nineteenth century, all of us are taking another look at this most maligned animal. We are beginning to shoot it not with guns but with cameras.

Europeans have had a more intelligent view for a good while. For years they have erected bat houses, like martin houses, in their backyards and in national forests to increase bat population for insect control. Abandoned mine shafts in Cornwall that contain bat colonies have been capped with special entrances and exits for bats.

Laws protect bats in Europe and Russia. Britain prohibits any unlicensed disturbance of bats or their roosts in either public or private premises. In this country, a vigorous organization, Bat Conservation International, works to educate the public and the press about bats and to legislate their protection.

Inevitably, man hates what he does not understand, and the night-flying bat, although the most numerous animal on earth, has been difficult to understand and admire. But like the Wizard of Oz, the bat as a threat and a terrorist is a humbug.

As a preventer of attic fires, a voracious eater of mosquitoes and other insects, and a pollinator and sower of plants, a bat is the nicest neighbor one could have. We continue to cherish and protect our attic full of them.

Hunters, Deer and Canada Geese

When we moved to Vixen Hill, the country was almost the country visualized in the old western saying: "When you can see the smoke from somebody else's chimney, the place is getting too crowded." For our first fifteen years we couldn't see anybody else's smoke.

Though such isolation has its joys, it also has its perils. Transients thought our land was unpopulated and, hence, the property of anyone who wished to come on it, particularly anyone who wished to come on it and hunt.

The prevailing game in those days was the ring-necked pheasant. Pheasants were so abundant that their hens ran everywhere, and you couldn't walk more than a hundred feet through a field without stirring up a cockbird. It would rise with crashing suddenness and, screaming, "Chottle, chottle, chottle, chottle, chottle," soar off to the next hedgerow.

Pheasants, being a form of wild chicken, were of a worthwhile size to shoot. Hunters walked along our roads and wandered onto any property that looked promising for game. No matter how the property owner posted his land, the hunters wandered on without a care. If they noticed the posting signs at all, it was to tear them down. Some didn't even bother to come in to hunt. They shot birds from a car on the road. This was both illegal and dangerous, but who was to stop them?

So, every day of hunting season, and especially on Saturdays, our farm sounded like a battlefield. Most of these hunters were gun-happy boobs who didn't know how to shoot and were wildly careless. Their hunting was a threat to our lives.

Mimi's concern was the pheasants. She didn't want them shot. So every weekend I had to go out, at considerable hazard, tell the hunters the property was posted and that they could leave or have a case made against them. I came to dread the weekends. I wanted to accomplish things that needed doing, and all I was managing was being a game warden. I was threatened with bodily harm, I had guns aimed at me and I endured lots of verbal abuse both profane and obscene.

I thought it over. There must be a better way to deal with the problem. It was then that John Kosky, a business client, asked me whether we had any pheasants. Kosky had come from Upstate New York and liked to hunt. Suddenly, I was inspired.

"Yes," I said, "I have pheasants. Lots of them. And I'll make a deal with you. You keep the property posted, and you may hunt all you like provided you keep the other hunters off."

"Okay. Can I brings friends to hunt?"

"If they're as careful and safe as you are and they'll help you do the job."

This stratagem converted an ordeal into a pleasant affair. Kosky, who turned out to be a dedicated naturalist as well as a crack shot, called each year two or three weeks before the small-game season opened to say he and a friend would be out to post the property. They worked at it for most of the day, then came in for a drink and a visit. Saturdays in hunting season, three or four hunters arrived with a hound and invited our setter to join in.

By definition, the hunters could, in small-game season, hunt pheasants, rabbits, squirrels, woodcock and quail, but they had no interest in anything but pheasant. In ten years I think the crowd shot only two rabbits. Automobiles killed more than that any week.

Then the great avian flu epidemic struck, beginning in the late sixties. Farmers were required to put down chicken flocks as large as twenty-five hundred because of infection. Even ducks and other fowl had to be destroyed.

Soon our hunters complained that we must be getting a lot of poachers because the pheasants had disappeared. You seldom heard a cockbird anymore. Even our basset hunts on Sundays, which once had raised cocks by the dozens, raised no more birds.

Considering it, I reasoned what had happened: the avian flu had killed off the pheasants. At first, everyone scoffed at the idea. It was easier to believe that overhunting had done it and that the flocks would come back. Now everyone accepts the explanation. More than twenty years after the epidemic, we still see few pheasants. I suspect natural restocking will take nearly fifty years in all, but it will occur. Our area is a natural habitat for pheasants.

Our hunters stopped coming out to hunt, but Kosky and one or two others came each year to post the property and to enjoy a country walk. John Kosky was an enthusiastic tracker, in addition to being a hunter. Until he moved back to New York State, he came regularly at all seasons to read the woodland, to find and follow deer slot and other spore, to observe our red foxes, woodchucks, possums, squirrels, chipmunks and even voles. During his last visit, he remarked that the deer population seemed to be increasing.

He was right.

∾

I have worked out a deer scenario that may or may not be correct. It goes this way. When we first moved out, we saw few deer except in Valley Forge Park. We saw them often there. The park, with its acres of grass, was almost entirely grazing land. The park was said to have two large herds, and we thrilled, as others did, at the sight. All of us paid obeisance to Bambi.

Then, in 1958, the Boy Scouts held a big international jamboree in

189

the park. Shortly afterward, deer began to appear on our basset hunts, luring the hounds off cottontails and leading them on long chases across country. I believe that the presence of the scouts in the park must have driven at least one herd up-country to seek quieter foraging. Once up here, and finding the area encouraging, the herd multiplied.

Soon we were seeing groups of six or eight deer browsing. One morning a ten-point buck jumped into the road ahead of my car when I was on the way to the station. When Kosky's hunting friends came out to post and walk, I sounded them on hunting deer. They weren't interested, being small-game people. They had no expertise in gutting and skinning an animal the size of a deer.

The deer were not yet a nuisance, but it didn't take them long. The growth of civilization, for which read population and development, has eliminated deer's natural predators. Once, pumas and other wildcats and wolves kept herds in check. These carnivores are gone. The only predators left are the hunter and the automobile. Hunters might have kept the balance dressed if most of the owners of large acreages were not still worshipping Bambi and forbidding deer hunting.

The high priests of Bambi and Thumper are mainly people who live in high-rise apartments or neat development houses and haven't a clue about what happens in the country. Animal overpopulations starve painfully, just as human overpopulations do. But no one publishes pictures of that in papers, and from a high rise you can't see it.

As for automobiles, they can hit and kill small animals with impunity, but hitting a deer is a close encounter of a lethal kind. A good many times the collision kills the driver and others in the car; in other collisions the car suffers major damage. Either way, the deer meets a brutal end.

∾

Certain plants and shrubs were supposed to be safe from deer foraging. Rhododendrons were supposed to be poisonous and other broad-leaved evergreens were said to be at least unattractive. The multiflora rose, with its murderous briers, might be tasty but objectionable to browse.

Not after the herds got big. Mountain laurel, primroses and azaleas were quickly eaten to the ground. Once the deer finished those, they tackled the rhododendrons. We lost about two dozen that we had planted on our woodland path. Mimi was understandably outraged.

Providence always seems to send answers to problems. This time the answer was Herb and Barbara Evans. They were expert hunters with bow and arrow, careful and expert naturalists.

Herb asked permission to hunt deer and I made with him the same deal I had made with John Kosky. He could hunt if he would keep the property posted and run other hunters off; I would agree not to let anyone else hunt without first referring the prospect to him.

That is the arrangement that prevails now. We are surrounded still by Bambi zealots, so the deer run off our property to avoid hunters. Even so, the deer are so numerous that each year Evans and the others permitted to hunt have killed six to eight deer. Herb always brings me the meat of the first deer, wrapped, frozen and marked. So I have a hundred pounds or so of venison to enjoy and bestow on friends. It is attractive from a dietary standpoint, for venison has little fat.

It would be nice to think this controls the deer, but it doesn't come close. We aren't even keeping even. Frequently I come home and find the area around my front door stinking like a zoo because the herd has been there. I see them browsing behind the house, comfortable and serene as a herd of sheep. Coyotes, which prey on young deer, are said to be heading our way. They could bring a solution—but also problems, as coyotes can kill pets and may attack small children.

∾

The Canada geese are threatening to become an equally severe problem, although they have been much longer evolving to it. When we first came out, Canada geese were a novelty. We measured the seasons by the times when their great, majestic V-shaped skeins flew over. When a gaggle of them settled on a local pond, everyone went to see. In those days we had more mallard ducks than geese.

I have puzzled over the steps in the transition. I recall that in our early days people like Mrs. Dick kept pilgrim geese, raising them for the table.

The few farm ponds in those days were abandoned graphite quarries infested with snapping turtles. So they were not attractive to wild geese except as brief resting places during migration.

A drought or two stimulated interest in putting in farm ponds, and these appeared everywhere. Meanwhile, domestic pilgrim geese crossed with migrating Canada geese, a union that raised some suspicion about the assumption that geese mate for life. That these crosses were taking place was evident in every gaggle. All kinds of mutations of the Canada markings appeared. The crossed geese had no urge to migrate. They found our local climate and many ponds most attractive, and fed bountifully in cornfields imperfectly gleaned.

The dominant strain in these crosses must have been the Canada strain because evidences of other strains disappeared and our local flocks soon looked to be completely Canada. I think, too, that a fair number of migratory geese elected to stay all year because, rapidly as geese multiply, our local flocks grew more rapidly than one would have expected from reproduction alone. Our winters have grown much warmer, too, from the huge amounts of heat man generates or a gradual warming of the climate or both.

So what is the problem?

A goose is the world's greatest manure machine. It eats at one end and evacuates from the other in almost a constant stream. As the flocks have grown, clean ponds have grown murky with manure. Every stretch of lawn and grass the geese cross becomes mucky.

Geese, when they feel in command of an area, grow aggressive. The ganders attack people with sustained animosity. At a minimum they can cause painful nips in long, single-minded assaults; at worst, as they come with spread wings, flailing in all directions, they can produce abrasions, contusions and even broken bones.

Geese create a traffic problem, for they cross a road in long parades. Plowing through such a parade will not damage a car, but it will ruin one's reputation as a caring person. The geese know this. Hence, these parades are slow and stately. Let the world wait, the geese seem to say, on our whim and convenience.

Finally, the geese have driven off our ducks. I have never seen a goose attack a duck, but I assume it must happen. Most of our mallards are gone, and the few I see avoid any pond where geese may be and seek the seclusion of small pools in streams.

I believe the number of resident geese in our area long ago exceeded five thousand, and each year it grows. Some predators of geese still inhabit our land. Such raptors as owls and hawks are numerous, and these prey on goslings, although few would have a chance against a full-grown goose. We also still have both red and gray foxes, which can tackle adult geese, but not nearly enough of them to make much of an impression on the population.

The goose problem must have grown widespread by now, for in 1993 the state spoke of establishing a season. To our bountiful venison supply we may soon be able to add roast goose.

INDIAN SUMMER

A Garden for the Table

Inevitably we were drawn into raising vegetables, but not as swiftly or as intensively in the beginning as we were later. World War II had put everyone through the Victory Garden drill. Once the war was over, many people were fugitives from Victory Gardens and the concept of raising one's own vegetables.

Our large freezer did encourage us to consider raising vegetables that could be frozen in quantity, but the quantities of lima beans, peas, and green beans we managed to raise and freeze were so pathetically small compared with the amount we ate that we resumed buying them. We liked corn, so Mimi planted eight stalks. That turned out to be just enough for the needs of birds, insects and blights. We got none. From this we learned that you can't grow corn in small quantities. For corn you need an acre or so, and a neighboring farmer can raise corn better and sell it to you cheaper than you can possibly do it for yourself. Our radishes were fine. Our carrots were not. We hadn't learned or been advised that when you grow carrots, you must be sure the bed is free of rocks. Carrots do not push rocks out of the way. Carrots just grow around them. We had maybe six carrots that looked like carrots. The rest looked like tired old men or cows' udders in interesting shades of orange.

∾

One thing Mimi did manage in those days, and I would say it typified her kind of gardening, was artichokes. For a while we had a slope that got a lot of sun. Mimi built a flight of steps down it, made rich beds on each side of the steps and planted globe artichokes. They grew to something resembling enormous thistles. The edible parts were the immature flowers of these monsters. They had thistlelike needles, and Mimi had to use gloves to harvest the chokes. But we had a good crop, and with lashings of melted butter, they were wonderful. In those days artichokes had elegant associations for me; I had seldom had them except at banquets in fine clubs and hotels.

This kind of exploration was the force behind much of Mimi's horticulture. She had never heard of a home gardener raising artichokes, so she was eager to learn whether one could. She shared my reluctance to do the obvious or the easy or the expected.

And though her adventure in tomatoes, when she undertook it, was an adventure into the commonplace, her method of doing it was on a fantastic scale.

Late in the 1950s the plant and seed people achieved an explosion of new types of tomatoes called Beefsteak, Jumbo Tom, Dombito, Big Guy and other grand names. They offered these miracles in deep red, medium red, orange and yellow. During this same season the rage for small tomatoes appeared: cherry and plum, notably. It became socially smart to garnish salad plates with deep red cherry tomatoes or greenish yellow plum tomatoes.

Mimi began her tomato adventure by planting the annual flower pockets on our terrace to cherry and plum tomatoes. She also explored varieties of full-size tomatoes. She bought seeds and flats and bedded out fifty plants each of two varieties. Such was the care of Mimi's planting that she seldom lost a plant. But when the season for outdoor planting arrived, Mimi worried. Her bedded tomatoes didn't look encouragingly hardy. Perhaps she ought to back them up with another two dozen plants. She planted a bed of these at one side of our terrace, making a five- by ten-foot patch.

Then her bedded seeds began to flourish. What to do with these? I suggested she get rid of some of them, but she felt tender about plants. She would neither kill a plant nor allow it to die. She dug a ten- by ten-foot patch in back of our house and planted her hundred plants, hoping a few would die on their own. None did.

By August we had a sea of tomatoes. The plants were not staked, so they sprawled all over each other. Harvesting them was a form of hopscotch. Soon I couldn't help but trample dozens of beauties for each dozen I harvested. We had tomatoes every meal. I preserved as many as I could as tomato juice, tomato sauce and whole tomatoes.

We couldn't give any away. In the tomato season in the country, the glut is everywhere.

During this tomato season Mimi did evolve one of the truly great tomato combinations: tomatoes sliced and lightly sprinkled with sugar, salt and pepper, doused with a good slosh of olive oil, splashed with tarragon vinegar, then liberally covered with finely chopped fresh basil from our herb garden.

We found another thing. The small tomatoes reseeded. Five or six years after we planted our annual pockets to cherry tomatoes, we still had volunteer plants. Even a fair number of full-size tomato plants came up and bore. I don't remember that the tomatoes from seed bore true, but the fruit was lovely and delicious.

❧

Work on our house, raising our sons, continuing my writing career in addition to a job that took ten hours per day, door to door: such pursuits drew us away from truck gardening. We were putting in trees and shrubs, and Mimi returned the annual pockets to begonias and, in later years, impatiens. So I mowed over our old garden plot and converted it to lawn.

It stayed lawn until the day my firm, an ad agency, fired me with virtually no warning. I had been with them for twenty years. The reason for the sudden severance was a political situation much too complicated to describe. I came home early on a lovely day in April feeling as if all of my blood had been drained out. Mimi was on our back lawn with our three sons, Wynn, who was twenty-four; Charles, seventeen; and Christopher, sixteen. I told them I had been fired. And I was ashamed to have been fired, though I didn't tell them that, and frightened and feeling old.

Mimi looked at me kindly and said: "Don't worry. We'll just have to start a garden."

We got into our work clothes and dug a fifty- by hundred-foot plot. With all of us working on it, we had a good time. By the end of the afternoon, I had worked off my despair. It is curious how encouraging sustained physical effort can be.

Mimi didn't worry how we would live. She was confident I would find a way to get enough money. This setback was, to her, a blessing. With me at home to help her, she could really experiment with the garden.

Her first step was to order enough three-year-old roots for five rows of asparagus. All of us liked asparagus. This planting should take care of us. In time it did, but we were fortunate not to have to depend on it in the beginning. Transplanted asparagus prospers slowly.

All of us liked spaghetti, so Mimi planted eight tomato plants, eight bell pepper plants and a long row of bermuda onions. We ate some of the produce fresh and still put by enough spaghetti sauce to get us through the winter.

Mimi had always wanted to try eggplants, so she raised four of those. The first year they bore well and Mimi could bestow the beautiful purple globes on her friends. The next year, all of the diseases and insects that attack eggplants got the news we were raising them, so we didn't get any more.

We had somewhat the same adventures with the members of the cabbage family that we liked: broccoli, cauliflower and Brussels sprouts. Our first crops were bountiful. The next year, the broccoli succumbed to worms. The year after a blight struck the cauliflower. The Brussels sprouts went on successfully for several years.

The Brussels sprouts fascinated us. They grew on this tall stalk that curved up like a cat's tail. The sprouts came out in buds along this stalk and expanded to about the size of Ping-Pong balls. In Philadelphia's Italian market, they sold Brussels sprouts on the stalk. Sprouts could take a great deal of cold weather. If there hadn't been a too-severe frost, we could pick enough for a meal into early December. Finally, though, a variety of small green worm invaded. The worms could be washed out and cleaned away, but it began to be too much trouble, and Mimi, who was now helping me on larger projects, stopped planting sprouts.

Mimi, a diligent reader of classified ads, found a combination of rental properties at a good price. We bought them. They were not producing much rent, so we decided to fix them up. I did the mechanical repairs, Mimi did the painting. She loved house painting. Presently, we had enough rentals to double our income. Then the prime rate went to 13 percent, and we were poor again. I had borrowed for them on a note on which the interest was prime plus 1 percent. When I borrowed, prime was 6 percent.

To cover the increase, I learned to be a bartender and worked at that for two years until I could build a substantial free-lance writing income, save money and invest in bonds. Soon I was making more than I had made at the agency, and Mimi could run her garden as a pleasure instead of a necessity.

∾

Mimi liked leeks for both their flavor and their association with Welsh mythology. Leeks weren't often available in market because there were too few British people about to create the demand. Mimi put in several rows of leeks, which are a two-year plant in the sense that they don't grow large enough for real eating until the summer of their second year. We boiled them and served them with butter like asparagus. They had a mild onion flavor and a nice texture. That year Mimi also raised elephant garlic, which she planted in the autumn and harvested the following August. It was impressive. The cloves were two and a half times the size of regular garlic. The flavor was somewhat milder.

One year Mimi put in a variety of hot peppers, enough, as it turned out, to burn out the southern half of Mexico. This was dicey stuff to fool with. The fruits, themselves, will burn you. I cast about for some use to make of these beauties because, no matter how hazardous they are, hot peppers, long, slender and sleekly scarlet or bright yellow or brilliant orange or green, smooth as baked enamel, are glorious sights. They cluster on their vines in abundance and give a sense of great riches.

The use I found was to remove their seeds, grind the peppers and soak them in cider vinegar for about a month. I then strained the liquid and ended with something a good deal hotter than Tabasco. Used in homeopathic amounts, this hyped juice gave a great zing to stews.

∾

After we bought our rental properties, redid them and got them rented out, Mimi embarked on yet another horticultural adventure. We had got a record of Michael Flanders and Donald Swann doing "At the Drop of a Hat," a song and patter presentation. In a number called "In the Bath" Flanders sang of raising the lordly loofah to scour his back and focused Mimi's attention on the fact that a loofah was something you could grow. It was the fruit of a plant. Were seeds available? They were.

Loofahs turned out to grow on vines, like zucchini, and the fruit was a gourd that looked like a zucchini but was several times larger. Beneath a sturdy green skin, the loofah had a network of spongelike material full of seeds. To get the scouring sponge, you peeled the fruit, let it dry, then shook out the seeds. It did make a fine scrubber.

The year Mimi grew loofahs, we had a large house for rent. A man who was publishing a new gardening magazine came to look at the house. He didn't take the house, but he sent a crew to do a story on loofahs. Presently, the *Wall Street Journal*, seeking a roundup of unusual plants people were growing in the summer of 1979, learned about Mimi's loofahs from the gardening magazine.

So Mimi made the front page of the June 19, 1979, *Wall Street Journal*: "Mimi Peeples of Chester Springs, Pa., explains the urge thus: 'I like to try something unusual every year.' She is growing a variety of gourd, *Luffa aegyptiaca* whose sponge-like pulp can be eaten fresh in salads or, when dried and peeled used as a cellulose scrubber for bathing or car washing." Loofahs were hard to top, so Mimi gradually drew away from the vegetable garden and turned to herbs.

Mimi

When she turned to herb gardening and dug her small plot beside our front terrace, it was about as large a garden as Mimi could manage. But herbs were not new to her.

Mimi had always been fascinated by herbs, and for good reason. Herbs are the most instantly rewarding of garden plants. They give you flavor, fragrance and a variety of flowers and unusual foliage all at the same time. Mimi had begun with mints and such plants as lemon balm and grown these along our lane beneath the ha-ha walls. She had grown basil each year to go with tomatoes and dill to go into potato salad and tarragon for béarnaise sauce.

She had grown borage and lovage and dittany of Crete and wormwood and, at one point, six varieties of scented geraniums. She grew and harvested oregano and sage.

Although she engaged in bigger enterprises, like loofahs, elephant garlic, horseradish and leeks, herbs ran through all of it like a leitmotiv in an opera. She grew regular thyme, woolly thyme and lemon thyme in our flagstone walks and hedged these walks with lavender, both pink and purple. All this, long before all the world discovered herbs.

So it was only fitting, when age and illness had reduced her energy, that Mimi should choose to work in an herb garden where she could have infinite riches in a small space.

When not working on her herb garden, Mimi sat on our front lawn and dug out wild strawberry plants and ground ivy with a kitchen fork. It was a pointless exercise. The plants came back. But it gave her a sense of accomplishment.

We were both members of what I regard as the generation of excess in America. Factory-made cigarettes, instead of roll-your-own, appeared when I was ten. Like most of my crowd, I became a smoker at sixteen and, presently, a heavy smoker. So did Mimi.

Both of us grew up under the influence of the Volstead Act and the Eighteenth Amendment, which imposed prohibition. When the Roosevelt administration abolished this absurdity, all of us felt compelled to begin a sustained celebration by drinking more than was healthy. Both Mimi and I did it. Being physically much larger than Mimi, I survived these excesses better than she.

Those were the days, too, when women felt the urge to maintain a slender, sylphlike figure. Mimi, who had a poor appetite anyhow, ate irregularly, often taking no food each day until she dined with the boys and me. Soon she was borderline anorexic.

Yet these were happy days. We grew adult in the years of great American writing, acting, art and music. We read the great books as they appeared and heard the great music and went to see the great theater. We grew up in what I now think, sadly, was the American flowering. Sadly, because I fear it has been over since 1970 or so.

As we do not see an age fade away, we do not see our loved ones age and waste away. No matter what alters them or how they are altered, they are still the lovely people we once knew. Because, by now, we know their manner and their soul, and these are the things we see rather than their looks.

☙

Mimi didn't sleep much. She stayed awake all hours, smoking and reading. She developed bursitis that had to be treated. I stopped smoking the year she put in her herb garden and urged her to do the same. She had a severe bronchial condition, her doctor said, a condition that would grow worse. Briefly, Mimi tried. She went for hypnosis and actually gave up cigarettes for eighteen months.

Then, perversely, she resumed.

One of her friends told me that Mimi hated herself and wanted to destroy herself. An early example had been her mixing the cement for our terrace walls and, despite the strenuous nature of the work, taking little more nourishment than the sherry she used to fortify herself.

Her habits took their toll. She broke both hips and had to have them replaced with metal. The cigarettes contributed to a severe arteriosclerosis that presently required two bypass operations. The bad diet wrecked her digestion and led to two operations for diverticulitis.

But she was still here at Vixen Hill, tough minded and durable, having opinions about everything we did, loving her three granddaughters, who adored her, teaching them herbs and allowing them to help her weed her herb garden. It was a lovely sight to see all of them working together.

She told them, too, about the mushrooms we had found and sent them looking for morels on Mother's Day, and about the leprechauns who lived beneath the thorn tree by the creek and kept a pot of gold there, and about the witch, called Madame Neufchâtel, who lived in the dead hickory in our swamp and came out on Hallowe'en, and about frogs and crayfish and bird feathers and why you must never kill a spider.

She made these the important things of their world as they had been the important things in hers.

From time to time, as she did these things, I looked at her to see her truly, instead of sensing the person I had always known. Her face had grown drawn, and her eyes had grown anxious. Her skin was sallow under her sunburn. Her step was uncertain, and she spent more and more time in bed.

She was in bed on our last Thanksgiving together. We sat and remembered our first one. We had moved to Vixen Hill on the Thanksgiving

weekend of 1946. It had been four days of the most glorious Indian summer weather with temperatures in the sixties. We had little money for food
and nothing to cook food in. So Mimi made our first Thanksgiving dinner
with four wieners cooked in an electric coffee percolator. They were the
most delicious wieners we ever tasted.

I had had to do most of the housekeeping for some time, but I did it
the ways Mimi had invented, so that everything was where she would
have put it and, when she came down occasionally to do things, nothing
would be strange to her. Because, really, if it were strange to her, it would
be strange to me, too. I only knew how to do it her way.

As Mimi declined, so did Bricket, our lovely setter bitch. She still
walked with me, but her step grew tentative, and I had to keep her close
beside me on the road lest she be killed. Her eyes were also anxious, as if
she asked:

"What am I not seeing? What am I not hearing?"

She got a severe nasal condition of congested breathing and constant
discharge. I took her to vets and bought lots of medicine. Nothing helped.

❧

At last Mimi developed osteoporosis of the spine, a disease excruciat-
ingly painful and incurable. As I understood the nature of it, the bones of
the spine commenced to erode to sharp edges that abraded the nerve
connections. The only relief came from painkillers that kept the patient
in a mild stupor.

Visiting nurses arrived, and mothers' helpers and therapists. They
walled me away from Mimi. They tried to persuade Mimi to give up smoking. She wouldn't. It was the last pleasure she had, she said, and if she
were going to die, she might as well have some comfort while she was
doing it.

The smoking combined with the constant lying in bed gave Mimi
pneumonia. The visiting nurse sent her to the hospital. There, she lay in
an oxygen apparatus heavily sedated and heavily wired with tubes, in a
semicoma. She began not to recognize us, to forget when we had been to
see her, to have no interest except trying to pull out the intravenous tubes
when she got a chance.

I spent a long time with her on her last afternoon. I didn't know it would be her last afternoon. One never knows things like that. I held her withered hand and looked into her blank and unseeing eyes.

"Would you like me to come back this evening and bring you something?"

Briefly her eyes lighted. And it was as if she was my girl again, all young and just starting out at Vixen Hill: "Yes," she said, "bring me a pack of cigarettes and a dry martini."

I squeezed her hand. "Of course," I said. "Lemon or olive?"

"Lemon."

∾

The phone rang at eight o'clock the next morning.

"This is Dr. Childs," a voice said. "Mimi died this morning at two."

You don't react immediately to news like this because it can't be true. If she had lived to the next St. Patrick's Day, we would have celebrated our forty-fifth wedding anniversary. Nothing that well established could be stopped by a telephone call.

Gradually the truth of it filled me. As I called the children and all of her friends I could think of, I knew it was true. But I couldn't cry. For some reason I couldn't cry.

I went down to find that Bricket had made messes and that my son Charles was busily cleaning them up.

"Bricket's in pretty bad shape," he said.

"Yes," I said, my mind not really on it. "I'm afraid she really should be put down."

Later that day I missed Bricket and asked Charles about her.

"I took her to the vet," he said. "I didn't think you needed her problems on top of everything else."

∾

The loss poured in on me when I began sorting through the things Mimi had accumulated during our forty-five years at Vixen Hill: saved cards and letters, small souvenirs from trips, dress patterns, plans for crewel and quilts, bright scraps of cloth and paper for Christmas decorations, small hoards of money tucked away in forgotten places. And I wept over them. So many sweet plans and small hopes unfulfilled.

But then they brought back memories, too. Once more Mimi was a tawny, coltish girl with the tawny Irish setter she had owned when I met her. Once more that lovely creature was back at Vixen Hill.

Distant Thunder

When we first moved to the country, our wave of arrivals must have dismayed the farmers whose families had tilled the soil for generations, farmers who had made their livings from dairies, orchards, mushroom barns, apiaries, poultry, hogs and cattle, and dirt farming. Chester County, Pennsylvania, was one of the most productive agricultural areas in the world, and one of the most diversified.

It seemed the ways of those farmers could not change and should not change. Theirs was the way of life our country loved. We doted on sleepy villages and long reaches of green pasture and white rushing waters and deep blue pools. We loved the sweet manure smell and the lowing that filled long milking barns and the clank of metal milk cans with mushroom tops. We admired the trees bent so heavy with ripe apples, their limbs had to be supported on crutches, the river of apples—deep red, light red, green, yellow and pink—flowing through the polishing and grading shed, the fresh cider, breathing attar of apples, cascading down the press. These were lovely things. Even our mushroom barns, dark caves of racked horse manure, dank and fetid and foggy but with pure white buttons of mushrooms scattered through the darkness, even these were precious to us.

Our narrow roads roamed as capriciously as a child on an errand. Two cars could pass on these roads, but just barely, and you were as likely to meet someone on horseback as another car, or someone walking, or cycling.

Not all of the houses were old. Many were, and all were seasoned with use. More important, they were far apart. Between them stretched space for field and forest, hill and ravine. It all looked sturdy. It proved to be delicate and fragile.

∞

Everybody idolized the bucolic life, so long as they didn't have to endure it. They liked to visit it and patronize it and say righteous things about protecting it while taking steps to destroy it.

The first really shattering step was, I think, the establishment of the dairy cooperative. Instead of getting milk from the dairy in cans, the cooperative picked it up in tank trucks. To participate cost each dairy farm $15,000 for new equipment in 1955 dollars.

Most dairy farmers didn't have that kind of money. They had to go out of business. The dairy farm across the road from us, where we bought our raw milk, was an early casualty. The one a mile down the road, to whom we went next, was a later casualty. Probably that was one object of the cooperative: to cut milk production by running a lot of little people out of business. After all, our country produced a great deal more milk than it could use.

Up stepped a savior for these little people: The real estate developer. He would take their dairy farms off their hands for a very high dollar, indeed. And triple his investment when he converted the land to houses. The relieved dairy farmer didn't care. He wasn't going to stay around. His school taxes were going up like a thermometer on a hot stove as the politicians used these taxes to force farms into the real estate development market. He was moving to Florida. No more freezing winter mornings for him!

Mimi and I had bought a large property because we really loved the land and were ready to suffer whatever trials were needed to hold and enjoy it. Our original neighbors also had large properties. We hoped this trend would continue.

Very soon, this seemed unlikely. The bought-up dairy farms began sprouting small houses on small plots of land. A song of the times called them "little boxes made of ticky tacky." These small holdings had lots of children whose parents immediately revolted against one-room schools that had no interior plumbing. These people were a ripe market for school jointures that consolidated the education of five to seven townships and a borough or two. They were ready to believe the absolute lie that is always used to sell every consolidation: It will be cheaper and, by implication, better.

It is never cheaper, and it is always a great deal worse.

When our jointure formed, our school tax was 32 mills on the assessed value of real estate. It rose gradually to 36 mills by 1966. In the next ten years, it doubled, then went to 74 mills in 1975. In 1976 the county reassessed all property. The new assessments were triple the old ones. In theory, the millage should have gone down substantially. Actually, it went down only seven mills for one year, 1976. The next two years it was back at 74 mills. In 1988 it was 127 mills. By 1993 it had risen to 208 mills. The school jointure proved to be an irresponsible taxing body that was never answerable to anyone but itself.

The steadily increasing taxes were needed, we were told, to provide a quality education. A quality education required football uniforms and all other equipment and supplies needed to play the game at a college level, plus the same for baseball, a stadium with lighting for night games, an Olympic-size swimming pool, auditoriums, cafeterias, large gymnasiums, band uniforms and instruments, a golfing instructor plus coaches for all of the other sports, a bus system that operated for only about fours hours a day but was large enough to meet the needs of a city. And so on and so on.

Maybe a quality education these days does require all of those things. It didn't when I went to school. We managed to finance some kind of second-hand uniforms for a football team that played its games in a public park. For any other sport, you found your own equipment and clothing. The band, being a part of the R.O.T.C., marched in government-issue uniforms. The members owned their own instruments. Our school had one huge assembly room designed to function as a theater, a cafeteria, an auditorium and a gymnasium, just as many private schools do now. Getting to school was our problem, not the school's. Those who could, walked. From farther distances, we rode bicycles. From great distances, our parents carpooled.

I got an education, and a good one. Judging by what comes out of the modern public schools, they seem to be little more than the most expensive baby-sitting operation the mind of man has ever conceived.

But say I'm dead wrong. Say it's all necessary. Should the expense of it all fall on the landholder, which still largely means the farmer? In 1976 the farmers in Chester County got some relief by entering a covenant that required the county to assess and tax farmland as farmland, not as prime building lots. Without this, floodplain had been assessed at $1,500 per acre. Who could afford to hold such land in order to sustain an essential part of the ecosystem?

The relief was temporary. On the one hand competition from such countries as Taiwan in growing such a crop as mushrooms toppled our county from being the number-one grower to third or fourth place. The amount of acreage needed to make a living from crop farming increased toward five hundred to one thousand acres.

Few farmers owned this much land. Those who wished to do crop farming had to lease arable fields wherever they could find them. Our arable land—we have only twenty acres of it—is in such a lease. I'm sure we could get more than the $25 a year per acre that we charge, but not enough to pay more than a fraction of the school taxes, a very small fraction.

∿

Any judge, any lawyer, any legislator who is honest about it will admit that the real estate tax is the most regressive tax ever devised. It is also the most attractive because it is the easiest to collect. All other assets and incomes can be moved or hidden. Land is immovable, and you can't hide it. So, although legislator after legislator in Pennsylvania, beginning in the 1960s, has run on strong promises to relieve the school tax on land, not one thing has been done about it. But talk.

I believe the real estate people are responsible for this failure. Far from wanting to encourage people to hold large parcels of land, they want to force as much land onto the market as possible. And skyrocketing school taxes are the best goad they can find to accomplish this. After all, even bad education is sacred.

Their scheming has been aided by the pressure of population growth. The 132 million people we had in our country in 1940 had grown to 249 million by 1990, an increase of 89 percent. The population of Pennsylvania in those decades grew from 9.9 million to 11.9 million, an increase of only 20 percent, and the population of Philadelphia actually declined from 1.9 million to 1.6 million. But the flight from the cities to the suburbs was so vigorous that, in the greater Philadelphia area, the population increased from 2.9 million in 1940 to 3.7 million in 1990, an increase of 28 percent.

These people had to be housed. They did not wish to live in the city. Ever-larger throngs poured into every countryside, seeking trees, greenery, fresh air and running water. Who could blame them? They were seeking the same things we had sought.

༄

But these lovely things cannot be had in small packages. The beautiful valley with its purling brook and the majestic hill with its stand of timber will no longer be beautiful after they are cumbered with two hundred houses. People who expect a scenic view will end up with the same view they had in town: the back or the front of somebody else's house. If that were all that happened, it still might be endurable.

But they will be cheated of other things far more critical. Their sewage systems will pollute the purling brook. Unless a central system with reservoirs is installed, there won't be enough water, and what there is will be polluted. They will have polluted it. With three and four cars and a lawn mower per household, they will have polluted the air as well.

༄

No one really plans the kinds of developments that pour upon us these days. Every developer builds his hundred or so houses as cheaply as possible, puts in as inexpensive paving and other facilities as he can get away with, gives no thought whatever to available police and fire protection, paramedical facilities, schools, capacity of feeder roads or anything else not directly on the site he is developing. His remedy for traffic congestion is to pave a half-mile of berm one lane wide along the front of his development. The resulting catastrophes are left for small, fairly helpless local governments to try to sort out. The whole adventure is a grand opera of unchecked greed.

And the greed feeds on itself. The more developments there are, the more people there are who want to live in the area. The more of these people who come, the more the price of land increases and the more people there are who buy land, not to enjoy it but to gamble on how high a price they can sell it for.

As an example of how tempting this can get, in 1946 we paid $250 per acre, or $16,250 for our sixty-five acres. By the late 1980s the pressure of development was so great that $30,000 per acre, or $1.95 million for the whole farm, would have been a low asking price. The question everyone asked was: "My God! Why don't you sell?"

As nearly as I could see it, the answer was: "And buy what with the money?" Or, in the words of the *Rubaiyat* of Omar Khayyám:

> *I often wonder what the Vintners buy*
> *One half so precious as the Goods they sell."*

I hope to spend my entire life on our farm and leave it for my sons and their children to spend their lives on. I hope all of us can resist the pressure to sell, even if a city rises around us, as it rose around the farms in upper Manhattan at the end of the last century.

More particularly, I could wish our governments would devise effective planning so that the people who are pouring in would at least find that they have bought something habitable with their money. That they won't find their water undrinkable, their sewage running down the gutters of their streets, their schools too small because nobody bothered to plan for a lot of new children, their safety jeopardized because there aren't enough firefighters or because the ambulances can't penetrate the traffic on roads that reach gridlock every morning and every evening.

It is idle to believe we can delay this growth more than temporarily with planning and zoning. Every generation yearns to build something, and this is an irrepressible urge. Moreover, as a breed, man is proliferating like rats and visiting ratlike waste on every bit of land he inhabits. If he does not amend his habits, he will presently render the earth entirely uninhabitable. For man. The rats will do fine.

∾

Nature, too, will survive. Amid our habitations, many wild animals thrive: deer, 'possums, skunks, foxes, muskrats, woodchucks, raccoons, rabbits, squirrels, chipmunks and birds. None of these residents need electricity or oil or gasoline or sewage. Whatever number of them a given place can support, live; the rest die. So their populations are always the right size.

Plants, from the smallest tender seedling to the largest oak or sycamore, endure forever, scattering millions of seeds in tumultuous showers of fecundity, year after year. Their roots push down walls and pull down houses and split the frost-eroded pavement and tap holes for rushing, eroding water to enter and flood. Among themselves the plants all fight for a place in the sun. Those that find it, live; those that fail, die. So their populations are always the right size.

I find some comfort in realizing that if the greed and stupidity of mankind demolish the beautiful natural world in which I have been privileged to live, nature has the strength to abate our nuisances after we are gone.

As this book shows a little, I have spent the years of my life watching the things of the earth, loving them and trying to participate without bringing too much damage. It has been rewarding enough that I would like to pass the joy along as far as it can reach.

Why bother? Why should I care?

Ralph Waldo Emerson wrote one of the loveliest answers to these questions in *The Rhodora*:

> ...Rhodora! If the sages ask thee why
> This charm is wasted on the earth and sky,
> Tell them, dear, That if eyes were made for seeing,
> Then Beauty is its own excuse for being...